the
poetry
of
Oscar
Wilde

ISBN

978 17 888 85140

the poetry of Oscar Wilde

This edition published in 2019 by Arcturus Publishing Limited
26/27 Bickels Yard, 151–153 Bermondsey Street,
London SE1 3HA

AD006521UK

Printed in the UK

Contents

Introduction 7

Helas! 11

Sonnet to Liberty 12

Ave Imperatrix 13

To Milton 18

Louis Napoleon..19

Sonnet 20

Quantum Mutata...21

Libertatis Sacra Fames 22

The Garden of Eros...23

Theoretikos 34

Requiescat 35

Sonnet on Approaching Italy 36

San Miniato..37

Ave Maria Gratia Plena..38

Rome Unvisited 39

Italia 42

Sonnet Written in Holy Week at Genoa 43

The New Helen...44

Urbs Sacra Æterna..48

Sonnet on Hearing the Dies Irae Sung
  in the Sistine Chapel 49

Easter Day..50

E Tenebris 51

The Burden of Itys..52

Vita Nuova 67

Impression du Matin 68

Madonna Mia 69

Magdalen Walks 70

Anathasia 72

Serenade for Music 75

Endymion for Music 77

La Bella Donna Della Mia Mente 79

Chanson 81

Charmides 82

Impressions 110

The Grave of Keats 112

Theocritus 113

In the Gold Room 114

Ballade de Marguerite 115

The Dole of the King's Daughter 119

Amor Intellectualis 120

Santa Decca 121

A Vision 122

By the Arno 123

Impression de Voyage 124

The Grave of Shelley 125

Fabien dei Franchi 126

Phêdre 127

Camma 128

Panthea 129

Impression: Le Reveillon 137

At Verona 138

Apologia 139

Quia Multum Amavi 141

Silentium Amoris 142

Her Voice 143

My Voice 145

Taedium Vitae 146

Humanitad 147

From Spring Days to Winter 165

The True Knowledge 166

Under the Balcony 167

The Harlot's House 169

Le Jardin des Tuileries 171

On the Sale by Auction of Keats' Love Letters 172

The New Remorse 173

Canzonet 174

In the Forest 176

To My Wife 177

Roses and Rue 178

Desespoir 181

Pan 182

The Sphinx 184

The Ballad of Reading Gaol 198

Ravenna 223

Index of First Lines 235

Introduction

Oscar Wilde was born Oscar Fingal O'Flahertie Wills Wilde in Dublin, Ireland on 16 October 1854. He was the son of Sir William Wilde, a prominent surgeon and author, and Jane Wilde, a progressive poet and mythological novelist who wrote under the alias Speranza. Oscar finished school at Portora Royal School in 1871 and attended Trinity College in Dublin and Magdalen College in Oxford between 1871 and 1878. During this time, he completed the long poem 'Ravenna', which won the prestigious Newdigate Prize in 1878. Much of his early inspiration came from two of his tutors, Walter Pater and John Ruskin, who analysed the role of art and aesthetics in life.

Wilde quickly developed a repuation for flamboyance. Journalists and playwrights turned him into a satirical figure in their works, and Wilde, happy to play along with the caricature, responded with the *Poems* of 1881, where he made fun of himself too. Over the next year, he lectured about art and beauty across the United States and Canada, where he was criticised for his extravagant clothing and exaggerated poses. Wilde married Constance Lloyd in 1884, and the couple had two children. During this time, he contributed numerous articles to a variety of magazines, including the *Pall Mall Gazette* and the *Daily Chronicle*, and even took on the editorship of the *Lady's World Magazine*, renaming it the *Woman's World*. At the same time, he continued to work on his fiction, leading to the publication of *The Happy Prince and Other Tales* in 1888.

In 1890, Wilde published one of his most famous works, *The Picture of Dorian Gray*. In this novel as well as in his wildly popular play *The Importance of Being Earnest* (1895), he criticised and satirised French decadence and Victorian ideals of society and beauty. His satirical plays, including *Lady Windermere's Fan* (1893) and *A Woman of No Importance* (1893), were some of his most successful works. Throughout his life Oscar Wilde delighted in composing poetry. This collection includes a range of his poetry, from the exotic verse of 'The Sphinx' to the hedonistic celebration of 'Panthea' to the more considered and even remorseful 'E Tenebris'. Though generally well received, his early poetry never reached the same heights as his better-known prose, with one exception, that he composed from bitter experience.

He began an intense and emotional relationship with Lord Alfred Douglas in 1891, but it soon drew the ire of Douglas's father, the Marquess of Queensberry. In 1894, he denounced Wilde for being homosexual. In response, Wilde sued for defamation, but the damage had already been done. In May 1895, the jury found Wilde guilty of sodomy. He was sentenced to two years' labour at Reading Gaol. While there, he wrote his final work, 'The Ballad of Reading Gaol', about his time in prison, which was published soon after his release. With his freedom restored, he moved to France to re-establish his reputation as an author, but in November 1900, he developed acute meningitis and died abruptly.

Helas!

To drift with every passion till my soul
Is a stringed lute on which all winds can play,
Is it for this that I have given away
Mine ancient wisdom, and austere control?
Methinks my life is a twice-written scroll
Scrawled over on some boyish holiday
With idle songs for pipe and virelay,
Which do but mar the secret of the whole.
Surely there was a time I might have trod
The sunlit heights, and from life's dissonance
Struck one clear chord to reach the ears of God:
Is that time dead? lo! with a little rod
I did but touch the honey of romance —
And must I lose a soul's inheritance?

Sonnet to Liberty

Not that I love thy children, whose dull eyes
See nothing save their own unlovely woe,
Whose minds know nothing, nothing care to know, –
But that the roar of thy Democracies,
Thy reigns of Terror, thy great Anarchies,
Mirror my wildest passions like the sea, –
And give my rage a brother – ! Liberty!
For this sake only do thy dissonant cries
Delight my discreet soul, else might all kings
By bloody knout or treacherous cannonades
Rob nations of their rights inviolate
And I remain unmoved – and yet, and yet,
These Christs that die upon the barricades,
God knows it I am with them, in some things.

Ave Imperatrix

Set in this stormy Northern sea,
Queen of these restless fields of tide,
England! what shall men say of thee,
Before whose feet the worlds divide?

The earth, a brittle globe of glass,
Lies in the hollow of thy hand,
And through its heart of crystal pass,
Like shadows through a twilight land,

The spears of crimson-suited war,
The long white-crested waves of fight,
And all the deadly fires which are
The torches of the lords of Night.

The yellow leopards, strained and lean,
The treacherous Russian knows so well,
With gaping blackened jaws are seen
Leap through the hail of screaming shell.

The strong sea-lion of England's wars
Hath left his sapphire cave of sea,
To battle with the storm that mars
The stars of England's chivalry.

The brazen-throated clarion blows
Across the Pathan's reedy fen,
And the high steeps of Indian snows
Shake to the tread of armèd men.

And many an Afghan chief, who lies
Beneath his cool pomegranate-trees,
Clutches his sword in fierce surmise
When on the mountain-side he sees

The fleet-foot Marri scout, who comes
To tell how he hath heard afar
The measured roll of English drums
Beat at the gates of Kandahar.

For southern wind and east wind meet
Where, girt and crowned by sword and fire,
England with bare and bloody feet
Climbs the steep road of wide empire.

O lonely Himalayan height,
Grey pillar of the Indian sky,
Where saw'st thou last in clanging flight
Our wingèd dogs of Victory?

The almond-groves of Samarcand,
Bokhara, where red lilies blow,
And Oxus, by whose yellow sand
The grave white-turbaned merchants go:

And on from thence to Ispahan,
The gilded garden of the sun,
Whence the long dusty caravan
Brings cedar wood and vermilion;

And that dread city of Cabool
Set at the mountain's scarpèd feet,

Whose marble tanks are ever full
With water for the noonday heat:

Where through the narrow straight Bazaar
A little maid Circassian
Is led, a present from the Czar
Unto some old and bearded Khan, –

Here have our wild war-eagles flown,
And flapped wide wings in fiery fight;
But the sad dove, that sits alone
In England – she hath no delight.

In vain the laughing girl will lean
To greet her love with love-lit eyes:
Down in some treacherous black ravine,
Clutching his flag, the dead boy lies.

And many a moon and sun will see
The lingering wistful children wait
To climb upon their father's knee;
And in each house made desolate

Pale women who have lost their lord
Will kiss the relics of the slain –
Some tarnished epaulette – some sword –
Poor toys to soothe such anguished pain.

For not in quiet English fields
Are these, our brothers, lain to rest,
Where we might deck their broken shields
With all the flowers the dead love best.

For some are by the Delhi walls,
And many in the Afghan land,
And many where the Ganges falls
Through seven mouths of shifting sand.

And some in Russian waters lie,
And others in the seas which are
The portals to the East, or by
The wind-swept heights of Trafalgar.

O wandering graves! O restless sleep!
O silence of the sunless day!
O still ravine! O stormy deep!
Give up your prey! Give up your prey!

And thou whose wounds are never healed,
Whose weary race is never won,
O Cromwell's England! must thou yield
For every inch of ground a son?

Go! crown with thorns thy gold-crowned head,
Change thy glad song to song of pain;
Wind and wild wave have got thy dead,
And will not yield them back again.

Wave and wild wind and foreign shore
Possess the flower of English land –
Lips that thy lips shall kiss no more,
Hands that shall never clasp thy hand.

What profit now that we have bound
The whole round world with nets of gold,

If hidden in our heart is found
The care that groweth never old?

What profit that our galleys ride,
Pine-forest-like, on every main?
Ruin and wreck are at our side,
Grim warders of the House of Pain.

Where are the brave, the strong, the fleet?
Where is our English chivalry?
Wild grasses are their burial-sheet,
And sobbing waves their threnody.

O loved ones lying far away,
What word of love can dead lips send!
O wasted dust! O senseless clay!
Is this the end! is this the end!

Peace, peace! we wrong the noble dead
To vex their solemn slumber so;
Though childless, and with thorn-crowned head,
Up the steep road must England go,

Yet when this fiery web is spun,
Her watchmen shall descry from far
The young Republic like a sun
Rise from these crimson seas of war.

To Milton

Milton! I think thy spirit hath passed away
From these white cliffs and high-embattled towers;
This gorgeous fiery-coloured world of ours
Seems fallen into ashes dull and grey,
And the age changed unto a mimic play
Wherein we waste our else too-crowded hours:
For all our pomp and pageantry and powers
We are but fit to delve the common clay,
Seeing this little isle on which we stand,
This England, this sea-lion of the sea,
By ignorant demagogues is held in fee,
Who love her not: Dear God! is this the land
Which bare a triple empire in her hand
When Cromwell spake the word Democracy!

Louis Napoleon

Eagle of Austerlitz! where were thy wings
When far away upon a barbarous strand,
In fight unequal, by an obscure hand,
Fell the last scion of thy brood of Kings!

Poor boy! thou shalt not flaunt thy cloak of red,
Or ride in state through Paris in the van
Of thy returning legions, but instead
Thy mother France, free and republican,

Shall on thy dead and crownless forehead place
The better laurels of a soldier's crown,
That not dishonoured should thy soul go down
To tell the mighty Sire of thy race

That France hath kissed the mouth of Liberty,
And found it sweeter than his honied bees,
And that the giant wave Democracy
Breaks on the shores where Kings lay couched at ease.

Sonnet

Christ, dost Thou live indeed? or are Thy bones
Still straitened in their rock-hewn sepulchre?
And was Thy Rising only dreamed by Her
Whose love of Thee for all her sin atones?
For here the air is horrid with men's groans,
The priests who call upon Thy name are slain,
Dost Thou not hear the bitter wail of pain
From those whose children lie upon the stones?
Come down, O Son of God! incestuous gloom
Curtains the land, and through the starless night
Over Thy Cross a Crescent moon I see!
If Thou in very truth didst burst the tomb
Come down, O Son of Man! and show Thy might
Lest Mahomet be crowned instead of Thee!

Quantum Mutata

There was a time in Europe long ago
When no man died for freedom anywhere,
But England's lion leaping from its lair
Laid hands on the oppressor! it was so
While England could a great Republic show.
Witness the men of Piedmont, chiefest care
Of Cromwell, when with impotent despair
The Pontiff in his painted portico
Trembled before our stern ambassadors.
How comes it then that from such high estate
We have thus fallen, save that Luxury
With barren merchandise piles up the gate
Where noble thoughts and deeds should enter by:
Else might we still be Milton's heritors.

Libertatis Sacra Fames

Albeit nurtured in democracy,
And liking best that state republican
Where every man is Kinglike and no man
Is crowned above his fellows, yet I see,
Spite of this modern fret for Liberty,
Better the rule of One, whom all obey,
Than to let clamorous demagogues betray
Our freedom with the kiss of anarchy.
Wherefore I love them not whose hands profane
Plant the red flag upon the piled-up street
For no right cause, beneath whose ignorant reign
Arts, Culture, Reverence, Honour, all things fade,
Save Treason and the dagger of her trade,
Or Murder with his silent bloody feet.

The Garden of Eros

It is full summer now, the heart of June;
Not yet the sunburnt reapers are a-stir
Upon the upland meadow where too soon
Rich autumn time, the season's usurer,
Will lend his hoarded gold to all the trees,
And see his treasure scattered by the wild and spendthrift
    breeze.

Too soon indeed! yet here the daffodil,
That love-child of the Spring, has lingered on
To vex the rose with jealousy, and still
The harebell spreads her azure pavilion,
And like a strayed and wandering reveller
Abandoned of its brothers, whom long since June's
    messenger

The missel-thrush has frighted from the glade,
One pale narcissus loiters fearfully
Close to a shadowy nook, where half afraid
Of their own loveliness some violets lie
That will not look the gold sun in the face
For fear of too much splendour, – ah! methinks it is a
    place

Which should be trodden by Persephone
When wearied of the flowerless fields of Dis!
Or danced on by the lads of Arcady!
The hidden secret of eternal bliss
Known to the Grecian here a man might find,
Ah! you and I may find it now if Love and Sleep be kind.

There are the flowers which mourning Herakles
Strewed on the tomb of Hylas, columbine,
Its white doves all a-flutter where the breeze
Kissed them too harshly, the small celandine,
That yellow-kirtled chorister of eve,
And lilac lady's-smock, – but let them bloom alone, and
    leave

Yon spired hollyhock red-crocketed
To sway its silent chimes, else must the bee,
Its little bellringer, go seek instead
Some other pleasaunce; the anemone
That weeps at daybreak, like a silly girl
Before her love, and hardly lets the butterflies unfurl

Their painted wings beside it, – bid it pine
In pale virginity; the winter snow
Will suit it better than those lips of thine
Whose fires would but scorch it, rather go
And pluck that amorous flower which blooms alone,
Fed by the pander wind with dust of kisses not its own.

The trumpet-mouths of red convolvulus
So dear to maidens, creamy meadow-sweet
Whiter than Juno's throat and odorous
As all Arabia, hyacinths the feet
Of Huntress Dian would be loth to mar
For any dappled fawn, – pluck these, and those fond
    flowers which are

Fairer than what Queen Venus trod upon
Beneath the pines of Ida, eucharis,

That morning star which does not dread the sun,
And budding marjoram which but to kiss
Would sweeten Cytheræ's lips and make
Adonis jealous, – these for thy head, – and for thy girdle
    take

Yon curving spray of purple clematis
Whose gorgeous dye outflames the Tyrian King,
And fox-gloves with their nodding chalices,
But that one narciss which the startled Spring
Let from her kirtle fall when first she heard
In her own woods the wild tempestuous song of
    summer's bird,

Ah! leave it for a subtle memory
Of those sweet tremulous days of rain and sun,
When April laughed between her tears to see
The early primrose with shy footsteps run
From the gnarled oak-tree roots till all the wold,
Spite of its brown and trampled leaves, grew bright with
    shimmering gold.

Nay, pluck it too, it is not half so sweet
As thou thyself, my soul's idolatry!
And when thou art a-wearied at thy feet
Shall oxlips weave their brightest tapestry,
For thee the woodbine shall forget its pride
And veil its tangled whorls, and thou shalt walk on
    daisies pied.

And I will cut a reed by yonder spring
And make the wood-gods jealous, and old Pan

Wonder what young intruder dares to sing
In these still haunts, where never foot of man
Should tread at evening, lest he chance to spy
The marble limbs of Artemis and all her company.

And I will tell thee why the jacinth wears
Such dread embroidery of dolorous moan,
And why the hapless nightingale forbears
To sing her song at noon, but weeps alone
When the fleet swallow sleeps, and rich men feast,
And why the laurel trembles when she sees the lightening
    east.

And I will sing how sad Proserpina
Unto a grave and gloomy Lord was wed,
And lure the silver-breasted Helena
Back from the lotus meadows of the dead,
So shalt thou see that awful loveliness
For which two mighty Hosts met fearfully in war's abyss!

And then I'll pipe to thee that Grecian tale
How Cynthia loves the lad Endymion,
And hidden in a grey and misty veil
Hies to the cliffs of Latmos once the Sun
Leaps from his ocean bed in fruitless chase
Of those pale flying feet which fade away in his embrace.

And if my flute can breathe sweet melody,
We may behold Her face who long ago
Dwelt among men by the Ægean sea,
And whose sad house with pillaged portico
And friezeless wall and columns toppled down

Looms o'er the ruins of that fair and violet-cinctured
    town.

Spirit of Beauty! tarry still a-while,
They are not dead, thine ancient votaries;
Some few there are to whom thy radiant smile
Is better than a thousand victories,
Though all the nobly slain of Waterloo
Rise up in wrath against them! tarry still, there
    are a few

Who for thy sake would give their manlihood
And consecrate their being, I at least
Have done so, made thy lips my daily food,
And in thy temples found a goodlier feast
Than this starved age can give me, spite of all
Its new-found creeds so sceptical and so dogmatical.

Here not Cephissos, not Ilissos flows,
The woods of white Colonos are not here,
On our bleak hills the olive never blows,
No simple priest conducts his lowing steer
Up the steep marble way, nor through the town
Do laughing maidens bear to thee the crocus-flowered
    gown.

Yet tarry! for the boy who loved thee best,
Whose very name should be a memory
To make thee linger, sleeps in silent rest
Beneath the Roman walls, and melody
Still mourns her sweetest lyre, none can play
The lute of Adonais, with his lips Song passed away.

Nay, when Keats died the Muses still had left
One silver voice to sing his threnody,
But ah! too soon of it we were bereft
When on that riven night and stormy sea
Panthea claimed her singer as her own,
And slew the mouth that praised her; since which time
    we walk alone,

Save for that fiery heart, that morning star
Of re-arisen England, whose clear eye
Saw from our tottering throne and waste of war
The grand Greek limbs of young Democracy
Rise mightily like Hesperus and bring
The great Republic! him at least thy love hath taught to
    sing,

And he hath been with thee at Thessaly,
And seen white Atalanta fleet of foot
In passionless and fierce virginity
Hunting the tusked boar, his honied lute
Hath pierced the cavern of the hollow hill,
And Venus laughs to know one knee will bow before her
    still.

And he hath kissed the lips of Proserpine,
And sung the Galilæan's requiem,
That wounded forehead dashed with blood and wine
He hath discrowned, the Ancient Gods in him
Have found their last, most ardent worshipper,
And the new Sign grows grey and dim before its
    conqueror.

Spirit of Beauty! tarry with us still,
It is not quenched the torch of poesy,
The star that shook above the Eastern hill
Holds unassailed its argent armoury
From all the gathering gloom and fretful fight –
O tarry with us still! for through the long and common
    night,

Morris, our sweet and simple Chaucer's child,
Dear heritor of Spenser's tuneful reed,
With soft and sylvan pipe has oft beguiled
The weary soul of man in troublous need,
And from the far and flowerless fields of ice
Has brought fair flowers meet to make an earthly
    paradise.

We know them all, Gudrun the strong men's bride,
Aslaug and Olafson we know them all,
How giant Grettir fought and Sigurd died,
And what enchantment held the king in thrall
When lonely Brynhild wrestled with the powers
That war against all passion, ah! how oft through summer
    hours,

Long listless summer hours when the noon
Being enamoured of a damask rose
Forgets to journey westward, till the moon
The pale usurper of its tribute grows
From a thin sickle to a silver shield
And chides its loitering car – how oft, in some cool
    grassy field

Far from the cricket-ground and noisy eight,
At Bagley, where the rustling bluebells come
Almost before the blackbird finds a mate
And overstay the swallow, and the hum
Of many murmuring bees flits through the leaves,
Have I lain poring on the dreamy tales his fancy weaves,

And through their unreal woes and mimic pain
Wept for myself, and so was purified,
And in their simple mirth grew glad again;
For as I sailed upon that pictured tide
The strength and splendour of the storm was mine
Without the storm's red ruin, for the singer is divine;

The little laugh of water falling down
Is not so musical, the clammy gold
Close hoarded in the tiny waxen town
Has less of sweetness in it, and the old
Half-withered reeds that waved in Arcady
Touched by his lips break forth again to fresher harmony.

Spirit of Beauty tarry yet a-while!
Although the cheating merchants of the mart
With iron roads profane our lovely isle,
And break on whirling wheels the limbs of Art,
Ay! though the crowded factories beget
The blind-worm Ignorance that slays the soul, O tarry yet!

For one at least there is, – He bears his name
From Dante and the seraph Gabriel, –
Whose double laurels burn with deathless flame
To light thine altar; He too loves thee well,

Who saw old Merlin lured in Vivien's snare,
And the white feet of angels coming down the golden
   stair,

Loves thee so well, that all the World for him
A gorgeous-coloured vestiture must wear,
And Sorrow take a purple diadem,
Or else be no more Sorrow, and Despair
Gild its own thorns, and Pain, like Adon, be
Even in anguish beautiful; — such is the empery

Which Painters hold, and such the heritage
This gentle solemn Spirit doth possess,
Being a better mirror of his age
In all his pity, love, and weariness,
Than those who can but copy common things,
And leave the Soul unpainted with its mighty
   questionings.

But they are few, and all romance has flown,
And men can prophesy about the sun,
And lecture on his arrows — how, alone,
Through a waste void the soulless atoms run,
How from each tree its weeping nymph has fled,
And that no more 'mid English reeds a Naïad shows her
   head.

Methinks these new Actaons boast too soon
That they have spied on beauty; what if we
Have analyzed the rainbow, robbed the moon
Of her most ancient, chastest mystery,
Shall I, the last Endymion, lose all hope

Because rude eyes peer at my mistress through a
    telescope!

What profit if this scientific age
Burst through our gates with all its retinue
Of modern miracles! Can it assuage
One lover's breaking heart? what can it do
To make one life more beautiful, one day
More godlike in its period? but now the age of Clay

Returns in horrid cycle, and the earth
Hath borne again a noisy progeny
Of ignorant Titans, whose ungodly birth
Hurls them against the august hierarchy
Which sat upon Olympus, to the Dust
They have appealed, and to that barren arbiter they must

Repair for judgment, let them, if they can,
From Natural Warfare and insensate Chance,
Create the new Ideal rule for man!
Methinks that was not my inheritance;
For I was nurtured otherwise, my soul
Passes from higher heights of life to a more
    supreme goal.

Lo! while we spake the earth did turn away
Her visage from the God, and Hecate's boat
Rose silver-laden, till the jealous day
Blew all its torches out: I did not note
The waning hours, to young Endymions
Time's palsied fingers count in vain his rosary of suns!

Mark how the yellow iris wearily
Leans back its throat, as though it would be kissed
By its false chamberer, the dragon-fly,
Who, like a blue vein on a girl's white wrist,
Sleeps on that snowy primrose of the night,
Which 'gins to flush with crimson shame, and die
    beneath the light.

Come let us go, against the pallid shield
Of the wan sky the almond blossoms gleam,
The corncrake nested in the unmown field
Answers its mate, across the misty stream
On fitful wing the startled curlews fly,
And in his sedgy bed the lark, for joy that Day is nigh,

Scatters the pearled dew from off the grass,
In tremulous ecstasy to greet the sun,
Who soon in gilded panoply will pass
Forth from yon orange-curtained pavilion
Hung in the burning east, see, the red rim
O'ertops the expectant hills! it is the God! for love of him

Already the shrill lark is out of sight,
Flooding with waves of song this silent dell, –
Ah! there is something more in that bird's flight
Than could be tested in a crucible! –
But the air freshens, let us go, why soon
The woodmen will be here; how we have lived this night
    of June!

Theoretikos

This mighty empire hath but feet of clay:
Of all its ancient chivalry and might
Our little island is forsaken quite:
Some enemy hath stolen its crown of bay,
And from its hills that voice hath passed away
Which spake of Freedom: O come out of it,
Come out of it, my Soul, thou art not fit
For this vile traffic-house, where day by day
Wisdom and reverence are sold at mart,
And the rude people rage with ignorant cries
Against an heritage of centuries.
It mars my calm: wherefore in dreams of Art
And loftiest culture I would stand apart,
Neither for God, nor for his enemies.

Requiescat

Tread lightly, she is near
Under the snow,
Speak gently, she can hear
The daisies grow.

All her bright golden hair
Tarnished with rust,
She that was young and fair
Fallen to dust.

Lily-like, white as snow,
She hardly knew
She was a woman, so
Sweetly she grew.

Coffin-board, heavy stone,
Lie on her breast,
I vex my heart alone,
She is at rest.

Peace, Peace, she cannot hear
Lyre or sonnet,
All my life's buried here,
Heap earth upon it.

Sonnet on Approaching Italy

I reached the Alps: the soul within me burned,
Italia, my Italia, at thy name:
And when from out the mountain's heart I came
And saw the land for which my life had yearned,
I laughed as one who some great prize had earned:
And musing on the marvel of thy fame
I watched the day, till marked with wounds of flame
The turquoise sky to burnished gold was turned.
The pine-trees waved as waves a woman's hair,
And in the orchards every twining spray
Was breaking into flakes of blossoming foam:
But when I knew that far away at Rome
In evil bonds a second Peter lay,
I wept to see the land so very fair.

San Miniato

See, I have climbed the mountain side
Up to this holy house of God,
Where once that Angel-Painter trod
Who saw the heavens opened wide,

And throned upon the crescent moon
The Virginal white Queen of Grace, –
Mary! could I but see thy face
Death could not come at all too soon.

O crowned by God with thorns and pain!
Mother of Christ! O mystic wife!
My heart is weary of this life
And over-sad to sing again.

O crowned by God with love and flame!
O crowned by Christ the Holy One!
O listen ere the searching sun
Show to the world my sin and shame.

Ave Maria Gratia Plena

Was this His coming! I had hoped to see
A scene of wondrous glory, as was told
Of some great God who in a rain of gold
Broke open bars and fell on Danae:
Or a dread vision as when Semele
Sickening for love and unappeased desire
Prayed to see God's clear body, and the fire
Caught her brown limbs and slew her utterly:
With such glad dreams I sought this holy place,
And now with wondering eyes and heart I stand
Before this supreme mystery of Love:
Some kneeling girl with passionless pale face,
An angel with a lily in his hand,
And over both the white wings of a Dove.

Rome Unvisited

I

The corn has turned from grey to red,
Since first my spirit wandered forth
From the drear cities of the north,
And to Italia's mountains fled.

And here I set my face toward home,
For all my pilgrimage is done,
Although, methinks, yon blood-red sun
Marshals the way to Holy Rome.

O Blessed Lady, who dost hold
Upon the seven hills thy reign!
O Mother without blot or stain,
Crowned with bright crowns of triple
    gold!

O Roma, Roma, at thy feet
I lay this barren gift of song!
For, ah! the way is steep and long
That leads unto thy sacred street.

II

And yet what joy it were for me
To turn my feet unto the south,
And journeying toward the Tiber mouth
To kneel again at Fiesole!

And wandering through the tangled pines
That break the gold of Arno's stream,

To see the purple mist and gleam
Of morning on the Apennines.

By many a vineyard-hidden home,
Orchard, and olive-garden grey,
Till from the drear Campagna's way
The seven hills bear up the dome!

III

A pilgrim from the northern seas –
What joy for me to seek alone
The wondrous Temple, and the throne
Of Him who holds the awful keys!

When, bright with purple and with gold,
Come priest and holy Cardinal,
And borne above the heads of all
The gentle Shepherd of the Fold.

O joy to see before I die
The only God-anointed King,
And hear the silver trumpets ring
A triumph as He passes by.

Or at the altar of the shrine
Holds high the mystic sacrifice,
And shows a God to human eyes
Beneath the veil of bread and wine.

IV

For lo, what changes time can bring!
The cycles of revolving years

May free my heart from all its fears –
And teach my lips a song to sing.

Before yon field of trembling gold
Is garnered into dusty sheaves,
Or ere the autumn's scarlet leaves
Flutter as birds adown the wold,

I may have run the glorious race,
And caught the torch while yet aflame,
And called upon the holy name
Of Him who now doth hide His face.

Italia

Italia! thou art fallen, though with sheen
Of battle-spears thy clamorous armies stride
From the north Alps to the Sicilian tide!
Ay! fallen, though the nations hail thee Queen
Because rich gold in every town is seen,
And on thy sapphire-lake in tossing pride
Of wind-filled vans thy myriad galleys ride
Beneath one flag of red and white and green.
O Fair and Strong! O Strong and Fair in vain!
Look southward where Rome's desecrated town
Lies mourning for her God-anointed King!
Look heaven-ward! shall God allow this thing?
Nay! but some flame-girt Raphael shall come down,
And smite the Spoiler with the sword of pain.

Sonnet Written in Holy Week at Genoa

I wandered in Scoglietto's green retreat,
The oranges on each o'erhanging spray
Burned as bright lamps of gold to shame the day
Some startled bird with fluttering wings and fleet
Made snow of all the blossoms, at my feet
Like silver moons the pale narcissi lay:
And the curved waves that streaked the sapphire bay
Laughed i' the sun, and life seemed very sweet.
Outside the young boy-priest passed singing clear,
'Jesus the Son of Mary has been slain,
O come and fill his sepulchre with flowers.'
Ah, God! Ah, God! those dear Hellenic hours
Had drowned all memory of Thy bitter pain,
The Cross, the Crown, the Soldiers, and the Spear.

The New Helen

Where hast thou been since round the walls of Troy
The sons of God fought in that great emprise?
Why dost thou walk our common earth again?
Hast thou forgotten that impassioned boy,
His purple galley, and his Tyrian men,
And treacherous Aphrodite's mocking eyes?
For surely it was thou, who, like a star
Hung in the silver silence of the night,
Didst lure the Old World chivalry and might
Into the clamorous crimson waves of war!

Or didst thou rule the fire-laden moon?
In amorous Sidon was thy temple built
Over the light and laughter of the sea?
Where, behind lattice scarlet-wrought and gilt,
Some brown-limbed girl did weave thee tapestry,
All through the waste and wearied hours of noon;
Till her wan cheek with flame of passion burned,
And she rose up the sea-washed lips to kiss
Of some glad Cyprian sailor, safe returned
From Calpé and the cliffs of Herakles!

No! thou art Helen, and none other one!
It was for thee that young Sarpedôn died,
And Memnôn's manhood was untimely spent;
It was for thee gold-crested Hector tried
With Thetis' child that evil race to run,
In the last year of thy beleaguerment;
Ay! even now the glory of thy fame
Burns in those fields of trampled asphodel,

Where the high lords whom Ilion knew so well
Clash ghostly shields, and call upon thy name.

Where hast thou been? in that enchanted land
Whose slumbering vales forlorn Calypso knew,
Where never mower rose to greet the day
But all unswathed the trammeling grasses grew,
And the sad shepherd saw the tall corn stand
Till summer's red had changed to withered gray?
Didst thou lie there by some Lethæan stream
Deep brooding on thine ancient memory,
The crash of broken spears, the fiery gleam
From shivered helm, the Grecian battle-cry?

Nay, thou were hidden in that hollow hill
With one who is forgotten utterly,
That discrowned Queen men call the Erycine;
Hidden away that never might'st thou see
The face of Her, before whose mouldering shrine
To-day at Rome the silent nations kneel;
Who gat from joy no joyous gladdening,
But only Love's intolerable pain,
Only a sword to pierce her heart in twain,
Only the bitterness of child-bearing.

The lotos-leaves which heal the wounds of Death
Lie in thy hand; O, be thou kind to me,
While yet I know the summer of my days;
For hardly can my tremulous lips draw breath
To fill the silver trumpet with thy praise,
So bowed am I before thy mystery;
So bowed and broken on Love's terrible wheel,

That I have lost all hope and heart to sing,
Yet care I not what ruin time may bring
If in thy temple thou wilt let me kneel.

Alas, alas, thou wilt not tarry here,
But, like that bird, the servant of the sun,
Who flies before the northwind and the night.
So wilt thou fly our evil land and drear,
Back to the tower of thine old delight,
And the red lips of young Euphorion;
Nor shall I ever see thy face again,
But in this poisonous garden must I stay,
Crowning my brows with the thorn-crown of pain,
Till all my loveless life shall pass away.

O Helen! Helen! Helen! Yet awhile,
Yet for a little while, O tarry here,
Till the dawn cometh and the shadows flee!
For in the gladsome sunlight of thy smile
Of heaven or hell I have no thought or fear,
Seeing I know no other god but thee:
No other god save him, before whose feet
In nets of gold the tired planets move,
The incarnate spirit of spiritual love
Who in thy body holds his joyous seat.

Thou wert not born as common women are!
But, girt with silver splendor of the foam,
Didst from the depths of sapphire seas arise!
And at thy coming some immortal star,
Bearded with flame, blazed in the Eastern skies;
And waked the shepherds on thine island home.

Thou shalt not die! no asps of Egypt creep
Close at thy heels to taint the delicate air;
No sullen-blooming poppies stain thy hair,
Those scarlet heralds of eternal sleep.

Lily of love, pure and inviolate!
Tower of ivory! red rose of fire!
Thou hast come down our darkness to illume:
For we, close-caught in the wide nets of Fate,
Wearied with waiting for the World's Desire,
Aimlessly wandered in the house of gloom,
Aimlessly sought some slumberous anodyne
For wasted lives, for lingering wretchedness,
Till we beheld thy re-arisen shrine,
And the white glory of thy loveliness.

Urbs Sacra Æterna

Rome! What a scroll of History thine has been!
In the first days thy sword republican
Ruled the whole world for many an age's span:
Then of thy peoples thou wert crownèd Queen,
Till in thy streets the bearded Goth was seen;
And now upon thy walls the breezes fan
(Ah, city crowned by God, discrowned by man!)
The hated flag of red and white and green.
When was thy glory! when in search for power
Thine eagles flew to greet the double sun,
And all the nations trembled at thy rod?
Nay, but thy glory tarried for this hour,
When pilgrims kneel before the Holy One,
The prisoned shepherd of the Church of God.

Sonnet on Hearing the Dies Irae Sung
in the Sistine Chapel

Nay, Lord, not thus! white lilies in the spring,
Sad olive-groves, or silver-breasted dove,
Teach me more clearly of Thy life and love
Than terrors of red flame and thundering.
The hillside vines dear memories of Thee bring:
A bird at evening flying to its nest
Tells me of One who had no place of rest:
I think it is of Thee the sparrows sing.
Come rather on some autumn afternoon,
When red and brown are burnished on the leaves,
And the fields echo to the gleaner's song,
Come when the splendid fulness of the moon
Looks down upon the rows of golden sheaves,
And reap Thy harvest: we have waited long.

Easter Day

The silver trumpets rang across the Dome:
The people knelt upon the ground with awe:
And borne upon the necks of men I saw,
Like some great God, the Holy Lord of Rome.
Priest-like, he wore a robe more white than foam,
And, king-like, swathed himself in royal red,
Three crowns of gold rose high upon his head:
In splendor and in light the Pope passed home.
My heart stole back across wide wastes of years
To One who wandered by a lonely sea,
And sought in vain for any place of rest:
'Foxes have holes, and every bird its nest,
I, only I, must wander wearily,
And bruise My feet, and drink wine salt with tears.'

E Tenebris

Come down, O Christ, and help me! reach Thy hand,
For I am drowning in a stormier sea
Than Simon on Thy lake of Galilee:
The wine of life is spilt upon the sand,
My heart is as some famine-murdered land,
Whence all good things have perished utterly,
And well I know my soul in Hell must lie
If I this night before God's throne should stand.
'He sleeps perchance, or rideth to the chase,
Like Baal, when his prophets howled that name
From morn to noon on Carmel's smitten height.'
Nay, peace, I shall behold before the night,
The feet of brass, the robe more white than flame,
The wounded hands, the weary human face.

The Burden of Itys

This English Thames is holier far than Rome,
Those harebells like a sudden flush of sea
Breaking across the woodland, with the foam
Of meadow-sweet and white anemone
To fleck their blue waves, – God is likelier there
Than hidden in that crystal-hearted star the pale monks
    bear!

Those violet-gleaming butterflies that take
Yon creamy lily for their pavilion
Are monsignores, and where the rushes shake
A lazy pike lies basking in the sun,
His eyes half shut, – he is some mitred old
Bishop in partibus! look at those gaudy scales all green
    and gold.

The wind the restless prisoner of the trees
Does well for Palæstrina, one would say
The mighty master's hands were on the keys
Of the Maria organ, which they play
When early on some sapphire Easter morn
In a high litter red as blood or sin the Pope is borne

From his dark House out to the Balcony
Above the bronze gates and the crowded square,
Whose very fountains seem for ecstasy
To toss their silver lances in the air,
And stretching out weak hands to East and West
In vain sends peace to peaceless lands, to restless nations
    rest.

Is not yon lingering orange afterglow
That stays to vex the moon more fair than all
Rome's lordliest pageants! strange, a year ago
I knelt before some crimson Cardinal
Who bare the Host across the Esquiline,
And now – those common poppies in the wheat seem
    twice as fine.

The blue-green beanfields yonder, tremulous
With the last shower, sweeter perfume bring
Through this cool evening than the odorous
Flame-jewelled censers the young deacons swing,
When the grey priest unlocks the curtained shrine,
And makes God's body from the common fruit of corn
    and vine.

Poor Fra Giovanni bawling at the Mass
Were out of tune now, for a small brown bird
Sings overhead, and through the long cool grass
I see that throbbing throat which once I heard
On starlit hills of flower-starred Arcady,
Once where the white and crescent sand of Salamis meets
    sea.

Sweet is the swallow twittering on the eaves
At daybreak, when the mower whets his scythe,
And stock-doves murmur, and the milkmaid leaves
Her little lonely bed, and carols blithe
To see the heavy-lowing cattle wait
Stretching their huge and dripping mouths across the
    farmyard gate.

And sweet the hops upon the Kentish leas,
And sweet the wind that lifts the new-mown hay,
And sweet the fretful swarms of grumbling bees
That round and round the linden blossoms play;
And sweet the heifer breathing in the stall,
And the green bursting figs that hang upon the red-brick
    wall,

And sweet to hear the cuckoo mock the spring
While the last violet loiters by the well,
And sweet to hear the shepherd Daphnis sing
The song of Linus through a sunny dell
Of warm Arcadia where the corn is gold
And the slight lithe-limbed reapers dance about the
    wattled fold.

And sweet with young Lycoris to recline
In some Illyrian valley far away,
Where canopied on herbs amaracine
We too might waste the summer-trancèd day
Matching our reeds in sportive rivalry,
While far beneath us frets the troubled purple
    of the sea.

But sweeter far if silver-sandalled foot
Of some long-hidden God should ever tread
The Nuneham meadows, if with reeded flute
Pressed to his lips some Faun might raise his head
By the green water-flags, ah! sweet indeed
To see the heavenly herdsman call his white-fleeced flock
    to feed.

Then sing to me thou tuneful chorister,
Though what thou sing'st be thine own requiem!
Tell me thy tale thou hapless chronicler
Of thine own tragedies! do not contemn
These unfamiliar haunts, this English field,
For many a lovely coronal our northern isle
    can yield

Which Grecian meadows know not, many a rose
Which all day long in vales Æolian
A lad might seek in vain for overgrows
Our hedges like a wanton courtesan
Unthrifty of its beauty; lilies too
Ilissos never mirrored star our streams, and
    cockles blue

Dot the green wheat which, though they are the signs
For swallows going south, would never spread
Their azure tents between the Attic vines;
Even that little weed of ragged red,
Which bids the robin pipe, in Arcady
Would be a trespasser, and many an unsung
    elegy

Sleeps in the reeds that fringe our winding Thames
Which to awake were sweeter ravishment
Than ever Syrinx wept for; diadems
Of brown bee-studded orchids which were meant
For Cytheræa's brows are hidden here
Unknown to Cytheræa, and by yonder
    pasturing steer

There is a tiny yellow daffodil,
The butterfly can see it from afar,
Although one summer evening's dew could fill
Its little cup twice over ere the star
Had called the lazy shepherd to his fold
And be no prodigal; each leaf is flecked with spotted gold

As if Jove's gorgeous leman Danaé
Hot from his gilded arms had stooped to kiss
The trembling petals, or young Mercury
Low-flying to the dusky ford of Dis
Had with one feather of his pinions
Just brushed them! the slight stem which bears the
    burden of its suns

Is hardly thicker than the gossamer,
Or poor Arachne's silver tapestry, –
Men say it bloomed upon the sepulchre
Of One I sometime worshipped, but to me
It seems to bring diviner memories
Of faun-loved Heliconian glades and blue nymph-haunted
    seas,

Of an untrodden vale at Tempe where
On the clear river's marge Narcissus lies,
The tangle of the forest in his hair,
The silence of the woodland in his eyes,
Wooing that drifting imagery which is
No sooner kissed than broken; memories of Salmacis

Who is not boy nor girl and yet is both,
Fed by two fires and unsatisfied

Through their excess, each passion being loth
For love's own sake to leave the other's side
Yet killing love by staying; memories
Of Oreads peeping through the leaves of silent moonlit
    trees,

Of lonely Ariadne on the wharf
At Naxos, when she saw the treacherous crew
Far out at sea, and waved her crimson scarf
And called false Theseus back again nor knew
That Dionysos on an amber pard
Was close behind her; memories of what Mæonia's
    bard

With sightless eyes beheld, the wall of Troy,
Queen Helen lying in the ivory room,
And at her side an amorous red-lipped boy
Trimming with dainty hand his helmet's plume,
And far away the moil, the shout, the groan,
As Hector shielded off the spear and Ajax hurled the
    stone;

Of wingèd Perseus with his flawless sword
Cleaving the snaky tresses of the witch,
And all those tales imperishably stored
In little Grecian urns, freightage more rich
Than any gaudy galleon of Spain
Bare from the Indies ever! these at least bring
    back again,

For well I know they are not dead at all,
The ancient Gods of Grecian poesy:

They are asleep, and when they hear thee call
Will wake and think 't is very Thessaly,
This Thames the Daulian waters, this cool glade
The yellow-irised mead where once young Itys laughed
    and played.

If it was thou dear jasmine-cradled bird
Who from the leafy stillness of thy throne
Sang to the wondrous boy, until he heard
The horn of Atalanta faintly blown
Across the Cumnor hills, and wandering
Through Bagley wood at evening found the Attic poets'
    spring, —

Ah! tiny sober-suited advocate
That pleadest for the moon against the day!
If thou didst make the shepherd seek his mate
On that sweet questing, when Proserpina
Forgot it was not Sicily and leant
Across the mossy Sandford stile in ravished
    wonderment, —

Light-winged and bright-eyed miracle of the wood!
If ever thou didst soothe with melody
One of that little clan, that brotherhood
Which loved the morning-star of Tuscany
More than the perfect sun of Raphael
And is immortal, sing to me! for I too love
    thee well.

Sing on! sing on! let the dull world grow young,
Let elemental things take form again,

And the old shapes of Beauty walk among
The simple garths and open crofts, as when
The son of Leto bare the willow rod,
And the soft sheep and shaggy goats followed the boyish
    God.

Sing on! sing on! and Bacchus will be here
Astride upon his gorgeous Indian throne,
And over whimpering tigers shake the spear
With yellow ivy crowned and gummy cone,
While at his side the wanton Bassarid
Will throw the lion by the mane and catch the mountain
    kid!

Sing on! and I will wear the leopard skin,
And steal the moonèd wings of Ashtaroth,
Upon whose icy chariot we could win
Cithæron in an hour e're the froth
Has over-brimmed the wine-vat or the Faun
Ceased from the treading! ay, before the flickering lamp of
    dawn

Has scared the hooting owlet to its nest,
And warned the bat to close its filmy vans,
Some Mænad girl with vine-leaves on her breast
Will filch their beech-nuts from the sleeping Pans
So softly that the little nested thrush
Will never wake, and then with shrilly laugh and leap will
    rush

Down the green valley where the fallen dew
Lies thick beneath the elm and count her store,

Till the brown Satyrs in a jolly crew
Trample the loosestrife down along the shore,
And where their hornèd master sits in state
Bring strawberries and bloomy plums upon a wicker
    crate!

Sing on! and soon with passion-wearied face
Through the cool leaves Apollo's lad will come,
The Tyrian prince his bristled boar will chase
Adown the chestnut-copses all a-bloom,
And ivory-limbed, grey-eyed, with look of pride,
After yon velvet-coated deer the virgin maid
    will ride.

Sing on! and I the dying boy will see
Stain with his purple blood the waxen bell
That overweighs the jacinth, and to me
The wretched Cyprian her woe will tell,
And I will kiss her mouth and streaming eyes,
And lead her to the myrtle-hidden grove where
    Adon lies!

Cry out aloud on Itys! memory
That foster-brother of remorse and pain
Drops poison in mine ear, – O to be free,
To burn one's old ships! and to launch again
Into the white-plumed battle of the waves
And fight old Proteus for the spoil of coral-flowered
    caves!

O for Medea with her poppied spell!
O for the secret of the Colchian shrine!

O for one leaf of that pale asphodel
Which binds the tired brows of Proserpine,
And sheds such wondrous dews at eve that she
Dreams of the fields of Enna, by the far Sicilian sea,

Where oft the golden-girdled bee she chased
From lily to lily on the level mead,
Ere yet her sombre Lord had bid her taste
The deadly fruit of that pomegranate seed,
Ere the black steeds had harried her away
Down to the faint and flowerless land, the sick and
    sunless day.

O for one midnight and as paramour
The Venus of the little Melian farm!
O that some antique statue for one hour
Might wake to passion, and that I could charm
The Dawn at Florence from its dumb despair,
Mix with those mighty limbs and make that giant breast
    my lair!

Sing on! sing on! I would be drunk with life,
Drunk with the trampled vintage of my youth,
I would forget the wearying wasted strife,
The riven veil, the Gorgon eyes of Truth,
The prayerless vigil and the cry for prayer,
The barren gifts, the lifted arms, the dull insensate air!

Sing on! sing on! O feathered Niobe,
Thou canst make sorrow beautiful, and steal
From joy its sweetest music, not as we
Who by dead voiceless silence strive to heal

Our too untented wounds, and do but keep
Pain barricadoed in our hearts, and murder
  pillowed sleep.

Sing louder yet, why must I still behold
The wan white face of that deserted Christ,
Whose bleeding hands my hands did once enfold,
Whose smitten lips my lips so oft have kissed,
And now in mute and marble misery
Sits in his lone dishonoured House and weeps,
  perchance for me?

O Memory cast down thy wreathèd shell!
Break thy hoarse lute O sad Melpomene!
O Sorrow, Sorrow keep thy cloistered cell
Nor dim with tears this limpid Castaly!
Cease, cease, sad bird, thou dost the forest wrong
To vex its sylvan quiet with such wild impassioned song!

Cease, cease, or if 'tis anguish to be dumb
Take from the pastoral thrush her simpler air,
Whose jocund carelessness doth more become
This English woodland than thy keen despair,
Ah! cease and let the north wind bear thy lay
Back to the rocky hills of Thrace, the stormyDaulian bay.

A moment more, the startled leaves had stirred,
Endymion would have passed across the mead
Moonstruck with love, and this still Thames had heard
Pan plash and paddle groping for some reed
To lure from her blue cave that Naiad maid
Who for such piping listens half in joy and half afraid.

A moment more, the waking dove had cooed,
The silver daughter of the silver sea
With the fond gyves of clinging hands had wooed
Her wanton from the chase, and Dryope
Had thrust aside the branches of her oak
To see the lusty gold-haired lad rein in his snorting yoke.

A moment more, the trees had stooped to kiss
Pale Daphne just awakening from the swoon
Of tremulous laurels, lonely Salmacis
Had bared his barren beauty to the moon,
And through the vale with sad voluptuous smile
Antinous had wandered, the red lotus of the Nile

Down leaning from his black and clustering hair,
To shade those slumberous eyelids' caverned bliss,
Or else on yonder grassy slope with bare
High-tuniced limbs unravished Artemis
Had bade her hounds give tongue, and roused the deer
From his green ambuscade with shrill halloo and pricking
    spear.

Lie still, lie still, O passionate heart, lie still!
O Melancholy, fold thy raven wing!
O sobbing Dryad, from thy hollow hill
Come not with such despondent answering!
No more thou wingèd Marsyas complain,
Apollo loveth not to hear such troubled songs
    of pain!

It was a dream, the glade is tenantless,
No soft Ionian laughter moves the air,

The Thames creeps on in sluggish leadenness,
And from the copse left desolate and bare
Fled is young Bacchus with his revelry,
Yet still from Nuneham wood there comes that
    thrilling melody

So sad, that one might think a human heart
Brake in each separate note, a quality
Which music sometimes has, being the Art
Which is most nigh to tears and memory;
Poor mourning Philomel, what dost thou fear?
Thy sister doth not haunt these fields, Pandion is
    not here,

Here is no cruel Lord with murderous blade,
No woven web of bloody heraldries,
But mossy dells for roving comrades made,
Warm valleys where the tired student lies
With half-shut book, and many a winding walk
Where rustic lovers stray at eve in happy simple talk.

The harmless rabbit gambols with its young
Across the trampled towing-path, where late
A troop of laughing boys in jostling throng
Cheered with their noisy cries the racing eight;
The gossamer, with ravelled silver threads,
Works at its little loom, and from the dusky
    red-eaved sheds

Of the lone Farm a flickering light shines out
Where the swinked shepherd drives his bleating
    flock

Back to their wattled sheep-cotes, a faint shout
Comes from some Oxford boat at Sandford lock,
And starts the moor-hen from the sedgy rill,
And the dim lengthening shadows flit like swallows
    up the hill.

The heron passes homeward to the mere,
The blue mist creeps among the shivering trees,
Gold world by world the silent stars appear,
And like a blossom blown before the breeze
A white moon drifts across the shimmering sky,
Mute arbitress of all thy sad, thy rapturous threnody.

She does not heed thee, wherefore should she heed,
She knows Endymion is not far away;
'Tis I, 'tis I, whose soul is as the reed
Which has no message of its own to play,
So pipes another's bidding, it is I,
Drifting with every wind on the wide sea of
    misery.

Ah! the brown bird has ceased: one exquisite trill
About the sombre woodland seems to cling
Dying in music, else the air is still,
So still that one might hear the bat's small wing
Wander and wheel above the pines, or tell
Each tiny dew-drop dripping from the bluebell's
    brimming cell.

And far away across the lengthening wold,
Across the willowy flats and thickets brown,
Magdalen's tall tower tipped with tremulous gold

Marks the long High Street of the little town,
And warns me to return; I must not wait,
Hark! 'tis the curfew booming from the bell at Christ
    Church gate.

Vita Nuova

I stood by the unvintageable sea
Till the wet waves drenched face and hair with spray,
The long red fires of the dying day
Burned in the west; the wind piped drearily;
And to the land the clamorous gulls did flee:
'Alas!' I cried, 'my life is full of pain,
And who can garner fruit or golden grain,
From these waste fields which travail ceaselessly!'
My nets gaped wide with many a break and flaw
Nathless I threw them as my final cast
Into the sea, and waited for the end.
When lo! a sudden glory! and I saw
The argent splendor of white limbs ascend,
And in that joy forgot my tortured past.

Impression du Matin

The Thames nocturne of blue and gold
Changed to a Harmony in grey:
A barge with ochre-coloured hay
Dropt from the wharf: and chill and cold

The yellow fog came creeping down
The bridges, till the houses' walls
Seemed changed to shadows and St. Paul's
Loomed like a bubble o'er the town.

Then suddenly arose the clang
Of waking life; the streets were stirred
With country waggons: and a bird
Flew to the glistening roofs and sang.

But one pale woman all alone,
The daylight kissing her wan hair,
Loitered beneath the gas lamps' flare,
With lips of flame and heart of stone.

Madonna Mia

A lily girl, not made for this world's pain,
With brown, soft hair close braided by her ears,
And longing eyes half veiled by slumbrous tears
Like bluest water seen through mists of rain;
Pale cheeks whereon no love hath left its stain,
Red underlip drawn in for fear of love,
And white throat, whiter than the silvered dove,
Through whose wan marble creeps one purple vein.
Yet, though my lips shall praise her without cease,
Even to kiss her feet I am not bold,
Being o'ershadowed by the wings of awe.
Like Dante, when he stood with Beatrice
Beneath the flaming Lion's breast and saw
The seventh Crystal, and the Stair of Gold.

Magdalen Walks

The little white clouds are racing over the sky,
And the fields are strewn with the gold of the flower of
  March,
The daffodil breaks under foot, and the tasselled
  larch
Sways and swings as the thrush goes hurrying by.

A delicate odour is borne on the wings of the morning
  breeze,
The odour of deep wet grass, and of brown new-
  furrowed earth,
The birds are singing for joy of the Spring's glad birth,
Hopping from branch to branch on the rocking trees.

And all the woods are alive with the murmur and sound
  of Spring,
And the rosebud breaks into pink on the climbing
  briar,
And the crocus-bed is a quivering moon of fire
Girdled round with the belt of an amethyst ring.

And the plane to the pine-tree is whispering some tale of
  love
Till it rustles with laughter and tosses its mantle
  of green,
And the gloom of the wych-elm's hollow is lit with the
  iris sheen
Of the burnished rainbow throat and the silver breast of a
  dove.

See! the lark starts up from his bed in the meadow there,
Breaking the gossamer threads and the nets of dew,
And flashing a-down the river, a flame of blue!
The kingfisher flies like an arrow, and wounds the air.

Athanasia

To that gaunt House of Art which lacks for naught
Of all the great things men have saved from Time,
The withered body of a girl was brought
Dead ere the world's glad youth had touched its prime,
And seen by lonely Arabs lying hid
In the dim womb of some black pyramid.

But when they had unloosed the linen band
Which swathed the Egyptian's body, – lo! was found
Closed in the wasted hollow of her hand
A little seed, which sown in English ground
Did wondrous snow of starry blossoms bear
And spread rich odours through our spring-tide air.

With such strange arts this flower did allure
That all forgotten was the asphodel,
And the brown bee, the lily's paramour,
Forsook the cup where he was wont to dwell,
For not a thing of earth it seemed to be,
But stolen from some heavenly Arcady.

In vain the sad narcissus, wan and white
At its own beauty, hung across the stream,
The purple dragon-fly had no delight
With its gold dust to make his wings a-gleam,
Ah! no delight the jasmine-bloom to kiss,
Or brush the rain-pearls from the eucharis.

For love of it the passionate nightingale
Forgot the hills of Thrace, the cruel king,

And the pale dove no longer cared to sail
Through the wet woods at time of blossoming,
But round this flower of Egypt sought to float,
With silvered wing and amethystine throat.

While the hot sun blazed in his tower of blue
A cooling wind crept from the land of snows,
And the warm south with tender tears of dew
Drenched its white leaves when Hesperos up-rose
Amid those sea-green meadows of the sky
On which the scarlet bars of sunset lie.

But when o'er wastes of lily-haunted field
The tired birds had stayed their amorous tune,
And broad and glittering like an argent shield
High in the sapphire heavens hung the moon,
Did no strange dream or evil memory make
Each tremulous petal of its blossoms shake?

Ah no! to this bright flower a thousand years
Seemed but the lingering of a summer's day,
It never knew the tide of cankering fears
Which turn a boy's gold hair to withered grey,
The dread desire of death it never knew,
Or how all folk that they were born must rue.

For we to death with pipe and dancing go,
Nor would we pass the ivory gate again,
As some sad river wearied of its flow
Through the dull plains, the haunts of common men,
Leaps lover-like into the terrible sea!
And counts it gain to die so gloriously.

We mar our lordly strength in barren strife
With the world's legions led by clamorous care,
It never feels decay but gathers life
From the pure sunlight and the supreme air,
We live beneath Time's wasting sovereignty,
It is the child of all eternity.

Serenade for Music

The western wind is blowing fair
Across the dark Ægean sea,
And at the secret marble stair
My Tyrian galley waits for thee.
Come down! the purple sail is spread,
The watchman sleeps within the town,
O leave thy lily-flowered bed,
O Lady mine come down, come down!

She will not come, I know her well,
Of lover's vows she hath no care,
And little good a man can tell
Of one so cruel and so fair.
True love is but a woman's toy,
They never know the lover's pain,
And I who loved as loves a boy
Must love in vain, must love in vain.

O noble pilot, tell me true,
Is that the sheen of golden hair?
Or is it but the tangled dew
That binds the passion-flowers there?
Good sailor come and tell me now
Is that my Lady's lily hand?
Or is it but the gleaming prow,
Or is it but the silver sand?

No! no! 'tis not the tangled dew,
'Tis not the silver-fretted sand,
It is my own dear Lady true

With golden hair and lily hand!
O noble pilot, steer for Troy,
Good sailor, ply the labouring oar,
This is the Queen of life and joy
Whom we must bear from Grecian shore!

The waning sky grows faint and blue,
It wants an hour still of day,
Aboard! aboard! my gallant crew,
O Lady mine, away! away!
O noble pilot, steer for Troy,
Good sailor, ply the labouring oar,
O loved as only loves a boy!
O loved for ever evermore!

Endymion for Music

The apple trees are hung with gold,
And birds are loud in Arcady,
The sheep lie bleating in the fold,
The wild goat runs across the wold,
But yesterday his love he told,
I know he will come back to me.
O rising moon! O Lady moon!
Be you my lover's sentinel,
You cannot choose but know him well,
For he is shod with purple shoon,
You cannot choose but know my love,
For he a shepherd's crook doth bear,
And he is soft as any dove,
And brown and curly is his hair.

The turtle now has ceased to call
Upon her crimson-footed groom,
The grey wolf prowls about the stall,
The lily's singing seneschal
Sleeps in the lily-bell, and all
The violet hills are lost in gloom.
O risen moon! O holy moon!
Stand on the top of Helice,
And if my own true love you see,
Ah! if you see the purple shoon,
The hazel crook, the lad's brown hair,
The goat-skin wrapped about his arm,
Tell him that I am waiting where
The rushlight glimmers in the Farm.

The falling dew is cold and chill,
And no bird sings in Arcady,
The little fauns have left the hill,
Even the tired daffodil
Has closed its gilded doors, and still
My lover comes not back to me.
False moon! False moon! O waning moon!
Where is my own true lover gone,
Where are the lips vermilion,
The shepherd's crook, the purple shoon?
Why spread that silver pavilion,
Why wear that veil of drifting mist?
Ah! thou hast young Endymion,
Thou hast the lips that should be kissed!

La Bella Donna Della Mia Mente

My limbs are wasted with a flame,
My feet are sore with travelling,
For, calling on my Lady's name,
My lips have now forgot to sing.

O Linnet in the wild-rose brake
Strain for my Love thy melody,
O Lark sing louder for love's sake,
My gentle Lady passeth by.

She is too fair for any man
To see or hold his heart's delight,
Fairer than Queen or courtesan
Or moonlit water in the night.

Her hair is bound with myrtle leaves,
(Green leaves upon her golden hair!)
Green grasses through the yellow sheaves
Of autumn corn are not more fair.

Her little lips, more made to kiss
Than to cry bitterly for pain,
Are tremulous as brook-water is,
Or roses after evening rain.

Her neck is like white melilote
Flushing for pleasure of the sun,
The throbbing of the linnet's throat
Is not so sweet to look upon.

As a pomegranate, cut in twain,
White-seeded, is her crimson mouth,
Her cheeks are as the fading stain
Where the peach reddens to the south.

O twining hands! O delicate
White body made for love and pain!
O House of love! O desolate
Pale flower beaten by the rain!

Chanson

A ring of gold and a milk-white dove
Are goodly gifts for thee,
And a hempen rope for your own love
To hang upon a tree.

For you a House of Ivory,
(Roses are white in the rose-bower)!
A narrow bed for me to lie,
(White, O white, is the hemlock flower)!

Myrtle and jessamine for you,
(O the red rose is fair to see)!
For me the cypress and the rue,
(Finest of all is rosemary)!

For you three lovers of your hand,
(Green grass where a man lies dead)!
For me three paces on the sand,
(Plant lilies at my head)!

Charmides

I

He was a Grecian lad, who coming home
With pulpy figs and wine from Sicily
Stood at his galley's prow, and let the foam
Blow through his crisp brown curls unconsciously,
And holding wave and wind in boy's despite
Peered from his dripping seat across the wet and stormy
   night.

Till with the dawn he saw a burnished spear
Like a thin thread of gold against the sky,
And hoisted sail, and strained the creaking gear,
And bade the pilot head her lustily
Against the nor'west gale, and all day long
Held on his way, and marked the rowers' time with
   measured song.

And when the faint Corinthian hills were red
Dropped anchor in a little sandy bay,
And with fresh boughs of olive crowned his head,
And brushed from cheek and throat the hoary spray,
And washed his limbs with oil, and from the hold
Brought out his linen tunic and his sandals
   brazen-soled,

And a rich robe stained with the fishers' juice
Which of some swarthy trader he had bought
Upon the sunny quay at Syracuse,
And was with Tyrian broideries inwrought,
And by the questioning merchants made his way

Up through the soft and silver woods, and when the
    labouring day

Had spun its tangled web of crimson cloud,
Clomb the high hill, and with swift silent feet
Crept to the fane unnoticed by the crowd
Of busy priests, and from some dark retreat
Watched the young swains his frolic playmates bring
The firstling of their little flock, and the shy shepherd
    fling

The crackling salt upon the flame, or hang
His studded crook against the temple wall
To Her who keeps away the ravenous fang
Of the base wolf from homestead and from stall;
And then the clear-voiced maidens 'gan to sing,
And to the altar each man brought some goodly
    offering,

A beechen cup brimming with milky foam,
A fair cloth wrought with cunning imagery
Of hounds in chase, a waxen honey-comb
Dripping with oozy gold which scarce the bee
Had ceased from building, a black skin of oil
Meet for the wrestlers, a great boar the fierce and
    white-tusked spoil

Stolen from Artemis that jealous maid
To please Athena, and the dappled hide
Of a tall stag who in some mountain glade
Had met the shaft; and then the herald cried,
And from the pillared precinct one by one

Went the glad Greeks well pleased that they their simple
    vows had done.

And the old priest put out the waning fires
Save that one lamp whose restless ruby glowed
For ever in the cell, and the shrill lyres
Came fainter on the wind, as down the road
In joyous dance these country folk did pass,
And with stout hands the warder closed the gates of
    polished brass.

Long time he lay and hardly dared to breathe,
And heard the cadenced drip of spilt-out wine,
And the rose-petals falling from the wreath
As the night breezes wandered through the shrine,
And seemed to be in some entrancèd swoon
Till through the open roof above the full and brimming
    moon

Flooded with sheeny waves the marble floor,
When from his nook up leapt the venturous lad,
And flinging wide the cedar-carven door
Beheld an awful image saffron-clad
And armed for battle! the gaunt Griffin glared
From the huge helm, and the long lance of wreck and
    ruin flared

Like a red rod of flame, stony and steeled
The Gorgon's head its leaden eyeballs rolled,
And writhed its snaky horrors through the shield,
And gaped aghast with bloodless lips and cold
In passion impotent, while with blind gaze

The blinking owl between the feet hooted in shrill amaze.
The lonely fisher as he trimmed his lamp
Far out at sea off Sunium, or cast
The net for tunnies, heard a brazen tramp
Of horses smite the waves, and a wild blast
Divide the folded curtains of the night,
And knelt upon the little poop, and prayed in
    holy fright.

And guilty lovers in their venery
Forgat a little while their stolen sweets,
Deeming they heard dread Dian's bitter cry;
And the grim watchmen on their lofty seats
Ran to their shields in haste precipitate,
Or strained black-bearded throats across the dusky
    parapet.

For round the temple rolled the clang of arms,
And the twelve Gods leapt up in marble fear,
And the air quaked with dissonant alarums
Till huge Poseidon shook his mighty spear,
And on the frieze the prancing horses neighed,
And the low tread of hurrying feet rang from the
    cavalcade.

Ready for death with parted lips he stood,
And well content at such a price to see
That calm wide brow, that terrible maidenhood,
The marvel of that pitiless chastity,
Ah! well content indeed, for never wight
Since Troy's young shepherd prince had seen so wonderful
    a sight.

Ready for death he stood, but lo! the air
Grew silent, and the horses ceased to neigh,
And off his brow he tossed the clustering hair,
And from his limbs he throw the cloak away;
For whom would not such love make desperate?
And nigher came, and touched her throat, and with hands
    violate

Undid the cuirass, and the crocus gown,
And bared the breasts of polished ivory,
Till from the waist the peplos falling down
Left visible the secret mystery
Which to no lover will Athena show,
The grand cool flanks, the crescent thighs, the bossy hills
    of snow.

Those who have never known a lover's sin
Let them not read my ditty, it will be
To their dull ears so musicless and thin
That they will have no joy of it, but ye
To whose wan cheeks now creeps the lingering
    smile,
Ye who have learned who Eros is, – O listen yet awhile.

A little space he let his greedy eyes
Rest on the burnished image, till mere sight
Half swooned for surfeit of such luxuries,
And then his lips in hungering delight
Fed on her lips, and round the towered neck
He flung his arms, nor cared at all his passion's will to
    check.

Never I ween did lover hold such tryst,
For all night long he murmured honeyed word,
And saw her sweet unravished limbs, and kissed
Her pale and argent body undisturbed,
And paddled with the polished throat, and pressed
His hot and beating heart upon her chill and icy breast.

It was as if Numidian javelins
Pierced through and through his wild and whirling brain,
And his nerves thrilled like throbbing violins
In exquisite pulsation, and the pain
Was such sweet anguish that he never drew
His lips from hers till overhead the lark of warning flew.

They who have never seen the daylight peer
Into a darkened room, and drawn the curtain,
And with dull eyes and wearied from some dear
And worshipped body risen, they for certain
Will never know of what I try to sing,
How long the last kiss was, how fond and late his
    lingering.

The moon was girdled with a crystal rim,
The sign which shipmen say is ominous
Of wrath in heaven, the wan stars were dim,
And the low lightening east was tremulous
With the faint fluttering wings of flying dawn,
Ere from the silent sombre shrine his lover had
    withdrawn.

Down the steep rock with hurried feet and fast
Clomb the brave lad, and reached the cave of Pan,

And heard the goat-foot snoring as he passed,
And leapt upon a grassy knoll and ran
Like a young fawn unto an olive wood
Which in a shady valley by the well-built city stood;

And sought a little stream, which well he knew,
For oftentimes with boyish careless shout
The green and crested grebe he would pursue,
Or snare in woven net the silver trout,
And down amid the startled reeds he lay
Panting in breathless sweet affright, and waited
    for the day.

On the green bank he lay, and let one hand
Dip in the cool dark eddies listlessly,
And soon the breath of morning came and fanned
His hot flushed cheeks, or lifted wantonly
The tangled curls from off his forehead, while
He on the running water gazed with strange and
    secret smile.

And soon the shepherd in rough woollen cloak
With his long crook undid the wattled cotes,
And from the stack a thin blue wreath of smoke
Curled through the air across the ripening oats,
And on the hill the yellow house-dog bayed
As through the crisp and rustling fern the heavy
    cattle strayed.

And when the light-foot mower went afield
Across the meadows laced with threaded dew,
And the sheep bleated on the misty weald,

And from its nest the waking corncrake flew,
Some woodmen saw him lying by the stream
And marvelled much that any lad so beautiful
    could seem,

Nor deemed him born of mortals, and one said,
'It is young Hylas, that false runaway
Who with a Naiad now would make his bed
Forgetting Herakles,' but others,
'Nay, It is Narcissus, his own paramour,
Those are the fond and crimson lips no woman
    can allure.'

And when they nearer came a third one cried,
'It is young Dionysos who has hid
His spear and fawnskin by the river side
Weary of hunting with the Bassarid,
And wise indeed were we away to fly:
They live not long who on the gods immortal
    come to spy.'

So turned they back, and feared to look behind,
And told the timid swain how they had seen
Amid the reeds some woodland god reclined,
And no man dared to cross the open green,
And on that day no olive-tree was slain,
Nor rushes cut, but all deserted was the fair
    domain,

Save when the neat-herd's lad, his empty pail
Well slung upon his back, with leap and bound
Raced on the other side, and stopped to hail,

Hoping that he some comrade new had found,
And gat no answer, and then half afraid
Passed on his simple way, or down the still and silent
   glade

A little girl ran laughing from the farm,
Not thinking of love's secret mysteries,
And when she saw the white and gleaming arm
And all his manlihood, with longing eyes
Whose passion mocked her sweet virginity
Watched him awhile, and then stole back sadly and
   wearily.

Far off he heard the city's hum and noise,
And now and then the shriller laughter where
The passionate purity of brown-limbed boys
Wrestled or raced in the clear healthful air,
And now and then a little tinkling bell
As the shorn wether led the sheep down to the mossy
   well.

Through the grey willows danced the fretful gnat,
The grasshopper chirped idly from the tree,
In sleek and oily coat the water-rat
Breasting the little ripples manfully
Made for the wild-duck's nest, from bough to bough
Hopped the shy finch, and the huge tortoise crept across
   the slough.

On the faint wind floated the silky seeds
As the bright scythe swept through the waving grass,
The ousel-cock splashed circles in the reeds

And flecked with silver whorls the forest's glass,
Which scarce had caught again its imagery
Ere from its bed the dusky tench leapt at the dragonfly.

But little care had he for any thing
Though up and down the beech the squirrel played,
And from the copse the linnet 'gan to sing
To its brown mate its sweetest serenade;
Ah! little care indeed, for he had seen
The breasts of Pallas and the naked wonder of the Queen.

But when the herdsman called his straggling goats
With whistling pipe across the rocky road,
And the shard-beetle with its trumpet-notes
Boomed through the darkening woods, and seemed to
    bode
Of coming storm, and the belated crane
Passed homeward like a shadow, and the dull big drops of
    rain

Fell on the pattering fig-leaves, up he rose,
And from the gloomy forest went his way
Past sombre homestead and wet orchard-close,
And came at last unto a little quay,
And called his mates aboard, and took his seat
On the high poop, and pushed from land, and loosed the
    dripping sheet,

And steered across the bay, and when nine suns
Passed down the long and laddered way of gold,
And nine pale moons had breathed their orisons
To the chaste stars their confessors, or told

Their dearest secret to the downy moth
That will not fly at noonday, through the foam and
surging froth

Came a great owl with yellow sulphurous eyes
And lit upon the ship, whose timbers creaked
As though the lading of three argosies
Were in the hold, and flapped its wings and shrieked,
And darkness straightway stole across the deep,
Sheathed was Orion's sword, dread Mars himself fled
down the steep,

And the moon hid behind a tawny mask
Of drifting cloud, and from the ocean's marge
Rose the red plume, the huge and hornèd casque,
The seven-cubit spear, the brazen targe!
And clad in bright and burnished panoply
Athena strode across the stretch of sick and shivering sea!

To the dull sailors' sight her loosened looks
Seemed like the jagged storm-rack, and her feet
Only the spume that floats on hidden rocks,
And, marking how the rising waters beat
Against the rolling ship, the pilot cried
To the young helmsman at the stern to luff to windward
side

But he, the overbold adulterer,
A dear profaner of great mysteries,
An ardent amorous idolater,
When he beheld those grand relentless eyes
Laughed loud for joy, and crying out 'I come'

Leapt from the lofty poop into the chill and churning
    foam.

Then fell from the high heaven one bright star,
One dancer left the circling galaxy,
And back to Athens on her clattering car
In all the pride of venged divinity
Pale Pallas swept with shrill and steely clank,
And a few gurgling bubbles rose where her boy lover
    sank.

And the mast shuddered as the gaunt owl flew
With mocking hoots after the wrathful Queen,
And the old pilot bade the trembling crew
Hoist the big sail, and told how he had seen
Close to the stern a dim and giant form,
And like a dipping swallow the stout ship dashed through
    the storm.

And no man dared to speak of Charmides
Deeming that he some evil thing had wrought,
And when they reached the strait Symplegades
They beached their galley on the shore, and sought
The toll-gate of the city hastily,
And in the market showed their brown and pictured
    pottery.

II
But some good Triton-god had ruth, and bare
The boy's drowned body back to Grecian land,
And mermaids combed his dank and dripping hair
And smoothed his brow, and loosed his clenching hand;

Some brought sweet spices from far Araby,
And others bade the halcyon sing her softest
    lullaby.

And when he neared his old Athenian home,
A mighty billow rose up suddenly
Upon whose oily back the clotted foam
Lay diapered in some strange fantasy,
And clasping him unto its glassy breast
Swept landward, like a white-maned steed upon
    a venturous quest!

Now where Colonos leans unto the sea
There lies a long and level stretch of lawn;
The rabbit knows it, and the mountain bee
For it deserts Hymettus, and the Faun
Is not afraid, for never through the day
Comes a cry ruder than the shout of shepherd
    lads at play.

But often from the thorny labyrinth
And tangled branches of the circling wood
The stealthy hunter sees young Hyacinth
Hurling the polished disk, and draws his hood
Over his guilty gaze, and creeps away,
Nor dares to wind his horn, or − else at the first
    break of day

The Dryads come and throw the leathern ball
Along the reedy shore, and circumvent
Some goat-eared Pan to be their seneschal
For fear of bold Poseidon's ravishment,

And loose their girdles, with shy timorous eyes,
Lest from the surf his azure arms and purple beard
    should rise.

On this side and on that a rocky cave,
Hung with the yellow-bell'd laburnum, stands,
Smooth is the beach, save where some ebbing wave
Leaves its faint outline etched upon the sands,
As though it feared to be too soon forgot
By the green rush, its playfellow, – and yet, it is a spot

So small, that the inconstant butterfly
Could steal the hoarded money from each flower
Ere it was noon, and still not satisfy
Its over-greedy love, – within an hour
A sailor boy, were he but rude enow
To land and pluck a garland for his galley's painted prow,

Would almost leave the little meadow bare,
For it knows nothing of great pageantry,
Only a few narcissi here and there
Stand separate in sweet austerity,
Dotting the unmown grass with silver stars,
And here and there a daffodil waves tiny scimitars.

Hither the billow brought him, and was glad
Of such dear servitude, and where the land
Was virgin of all waters laid the lad
Upon the golden margent of the strand,
And like a lingering lover oft returned
To kiss those pallid limbs which once with intense
    fire burned,

Ere the wet seas had quenched that holocaust,
That self-fed flame, that passionate lustihead,
Ere grisly death with chill and nipping frost
Had withered up those lilies white and red
Which, while the boy would through the forest range,
Answered each other in a sweet antiphonal counter-
    change.

And when at dawn the wood-nymphs, hand-in-hand,
Threaded the bosky dell, their satyr spied
The boy's pale body stretched upon the sand,
And feared Poseidon's treachery, and cried,
And like bright sunbeams flitting through a glade
Each startled Dryad sought some safe and leafy
    ambuscade.

Save one white girl, who deemed it would not be
So dread a thing to feel a sea-god's arms
Crushing her breasts in amorous tyranny,
And longed to listen to those subtle charms
Insidious lovers weave when they would win
Some fencèd fortress, and stole back again, nor thought it
    sin

To yield her treasure unto one so fair,
And lay beside him, thirsty with love's drouth,
Called him soft names, played with his tangled hair,
And with hot lips made havoc of his mouth
Afraid he might not wake, and then afraid
Lest he might wake too soon, fled back, and then, fond
    renegade,

Returned to fresh assault, and all day long
Sat at his side, and laughed at her new toy,
And held his hand, and sang her sweetest song,
Then frowned to see how froward was the boy
Who would not with her maidenhood entwine,
Nor knew that three days since his eyes had looked on
 Proserpine;

Nor knew what sacrilege his lips had done,
But said, 'He will awake, I know him well,
He will awake at evening when the sun
Hangs his red shield on Corinth's citadel;
This sleep is but a cruel treachery
To make me love him more, and in some cavern of the
 sea

Deeper than ever falls the fisher's line
Already a huge Triton blows his horn,
And weaves a garland from the crystalline
And drifting ocean-tendrils to adorn
The emerald pillars of our bridal bed,
For sphered in foaming silver, and with coral crownèd
 head,

We two will sit upon a throne of pearl,
And a blue wave will be our canopy,
And at our feet the water-snakes will curl
In all their amethystine panoply
Of diamonded mail, and we will mark
The mullets swimming by the mast of some storm-
 foundered bark,

Vermilion-finned with eyes of bossy gold
Like flakes of crimson light, and the great deep
His glassy-portaled chamber will unfold,
And we will see the painted dolphins sleep
Cradled by murmuring halcyons on the rocks
Where Proteus in quaint suit of green pastures his
    monstrous flocks.

And tremulous opal-hued anemones
Will wave their purple fringes where we tread
Upon the mirrored floor, and argosies
Of fishes flecked with tawny scales will thread
The drifting cordage of the shattered wreck,
And honey-coloured amber beads our twining limbs will
    deck.'

But when that baffled Lord of War the Sun
With gaudy pennon flying passed away
Into his brazen House, and one by one
The little yellow stars began to stray
Across the field of heaven, ah! then indeed
She feared his lips upon her lips would never care
    to feed,

And cried, 'Awake, already the pale moon
Washes the trees with silver, and the wave
Creeps grey and chilly up this sandy dune,
The croaking frogs are out, and from the cave
The nightjar shrieks, the fluttering bats repass,
And the brown stoat with hollow flanks creeps through
    the dusky grass.

Nay, though thou art a god, be not so coy,
For in yon stream there is a little reed
That often whispers how a lovely boy
Lay with her once upon a grassy mead,
Who when his cruel pleasure he had done
Spread wings of rustling gold and soared aloft into the
    sun.

Be not so coy, the laurel trembles still
With great Apollo's kisses, and the fir
Whose clustering sisters fringe the seaward hill
Hath many a tale of that bold ravisher
Whom men call Boreas, and I have seen
The mocking eyes of Hermes through the poplar's silvery
    sheen.

Even the jealous Naiads call me fair,
And every morn a young and ruddy swain
Woos me with apples and with locks of hair,
And seeks to soothe my virginal disdain
By all the gifts the gentle wood-nymphs love;
But yesterday he brought to me an iris-plumaged
    dove

With little crimson feet, which with its store
Of seven spotted eggs the cruel lad
Had stolen from the lofty sycamore
At daybreak, when her amorous comrade had
Flown off in search of berried juniper
Which most they love; the fretful wasp, that earliest
    vintager

Of the blue grapes, hath not persistency
So constant as this simple shepherd-boy
For my poor lips, his joyous purity
And laughing sunny eyes might well decoy
A Dryad from her oath to Artemis;
For very beautiful is he, his mouth was made to kiss;

His argent forehead, like a rising moon
Over the dusky hills of meeting brows,
Is crescent shaped, the hot and Tyrian noon
Leads from the myrtle-grove no goodlier spouse
For Cytheræa, the first silky down
Fringes his blushing cheeks, and his young limbs are
    strong and brown;

And he is rich, and fat and fleecy herds
Of bleating sheep upon his meadows lie,
And many an earthen bowl of yellow curds
Is in his homestead for the thievish fly
To swim and drown in, the pink clover mead
Keeps its sweet store for him, and he can pipe on oaten
    reed.

And yet I love him not; it was for thee
I kept my love; I knew that thou would'st come
To rid me of this pallid chastity,
Thou fairest flower of the flowerless foam
Of all the wide Ægean, brightest star
Of ocean's azure heavens where the mirrored planets are!

I knew that thou would'st come, for when at first
The dry wood burgeoned, and the sap of spring

Swelled in my green and tender bark or burst
To myriad multitudinous blossoming
Which mocked the midnight with its mimic moons
That did not dread the dawn, and first the thrushes'
    rapturous tunes

Startled the squirrel from its granary,
And cuckoo flowers fringed the narrow lane,
Through my young leaves a sensuous ecstasy
Crept like new wine, and every mossy vein
Throbbed with the fitful pulse of amorous blood,
And the wild winds of passion shook my slim stem's
    maidenhood.

The trooping fawns at evening came and laid
Their cool black noses on my lowest boughs,
And on my topmost branch the blackbird made
A little nest of grasses for his spouse,
And now and then a twittering wren would light
On a thin twig which hardly bare the weight of such
    delight.

I was the Attic shepherd's trysting place,
Beneath my shadow Amaryllis lay,
And round my trunk would laughing Daphnis chase
The timorous girl, till tired out with play
She felt his hot breath stir her tangled hair,
And turned, and looked, and fled no more from such
    delightful snare.

Then come away unto my ambuscade
Where clustering woodbine weaves a canopy

For amorous pleasaunce, and the rustling shade
Of Paphian myrtles seems to sanctify
The dearest rites of love; there in the cool
And green recesses of its farthest depth there is pool,

The ouzel's haunt, the wild bee's pasturage,
For round its rim great creamy lilies float
Through their flat leaves in verdant anchorage,
Each cup a white-sailed golden-laden boat
Steered by a dragonfly, – be not afraid
To leave this wan and wave-kissed shore, surely the place
    was made

For lovers such as we; the Cyprian Queen,
One arm around her boyish paramour,
Strays often there at eve, and I have seen
The moon strip off her misty vestiture
For young Endymion's eyes; be not afraid,
The panther feet of Dian never tread that secret glade.

Nay if thou wil'st, back to the beating brine,
Back to the boisterous billow let us go,
And walk all day beneath the hyaline
Huge vault of Neptune's watery portico,
And watch the purple monsters of the deep
Sport in ungainly play, and from his lair keen
    Xiphias leap.

For if my mistress find me lying here
She will not ruth or gentle pity show,
But lay her boar-spear down, and with austere
Relentless fingers string the cornel bow,

And draw the feathered notch against her breast,
And loose the archèd cord; aye, even now upon
   the quest

I hear her hurrying feet, – awake, awake,
Thou laggard in love's battle! once at least
Let me drink deep of passion's wine, and slake
My parchèd being with the nectarous feast
Which even gods affect! O come, Love, come,
Still we have time to reach the cavern of thine
   azure home.'

Scarce had she spoken when the shuddering trees
Shook, and the leaves divided, and the air
Grew conscious of a god, and the grey seas
Crawled backward, and a long and dismal blare
Blew from some tasselled horn, a sleuth-hound bayed,
And like a flame a barbèd reed flew whizzing down the
   glade.

And where the little flowers of her breast
Just brake into their milky blossoming,
This murderous paramour, this unbidden guest,
Pierced and struck deep in horrid chambering,
And ploughed a bloody furrow with its dart,
And dug a long red road, and cleft with wingèd
   death her heart.

Sobbing her life out with a bitter cry
On the boy's body fell the Dryad maid,
Sobbing for incomplete virginity,
And raptures unenjoyed, and pleasures dead,

And all the pain of things unsatisfied,
And the bright drops of crimson youth crept down her
    throbbing side.

Ah! pitiful it was to hear her moan,
And very pitiful to see her die
Ere she had yielded up her sweets, or known
The joy of passion, that dread mystery
Which not to know is not to live at all, And yet to know
    is to be held in death's most deadly thrall.

But as it hapt the Queen of Cythere,
Who with Adonis all night long had lain
Within some shepherd's hut in Arcady,
On team of silver doves and gilded wain
Was journeying Paphos-ward, high up afar
From mortal ken between the mountains and the
    morning star,

And when low down she spied the hapless pair,
And heard the Oread's faint despairing cry,
Whose cadence seemed to play upon the air
As though it were a viol, hastily
She bade her pigeons fold each straining plume,
And dropt to earth, and reached the strand, and saw their
    dolorous doom.

For as a gardener turning back his head
To catch the last notes of the linnet, mows
With careless scythe too near some flower bed,
And cuts the thorny pillar of the rose,
And with the flower's loosened loneliness

Strews the brown mould; or as some shepherd lad in
    wantonness

Driving his little flock along the mead
Treads down two daffodils, which side by side
Have lured the lady-bird with yellow brede
And made the gaudy moth forget its pride,
Treads down their brimming golden chalices
Under light feet which were not made for such rude
    ravages;

Or as a schoolboy tired of his book
Flings himself down upon the reedy grass
And plucks two water-lilies from the brook,
And for a time forgets the hour glass,
Then wearies of their sweets, and goes his way,
And lets the hot sun kill them, even so these loverslay.

And Venus cried, 'It is dread Artemis
Whose bitter hand hath wrought this cruelty,
Or else that mightier maid whose care it is
To guard her strong and stainless majesty
Upon the hill Athenian, — alas!
That they who loved so well unloved into Death's house
    should pass.'

So with soft hands she laid the boy and girl
In the great golden waggon tenderly
(Her white throat whiter than a moony pearl
Just threaded with a blue vein's tapestry
Had not yet ceased to throb, and still her breast
Swayed like a wind-stirred lily in ambiguous unrest)

And then each pigeon spread its milky van,
The bright car soared into the dawning sky,
And like a cloud the aerial caravan
Passed over the Ægean silently,
Till the faint air was troubled with the song
From the wan mouths that call on bleeding Thammuz
    all night long.

But when the doves had reached their wonted goal
Where the wide stair of orbèd marble dips
Its snows into the sea, her fluttering soul
Just shook the trembling petals of her lips
And passed into the void, and Venus knew
That one fair maid the less would walk amid her
    retinue,

And bade her servants carve a cedar chest
With all the wonder of this history,
Within whose scented womb their limbs should rest
Where olive-trees make tender the blue sky
On the low hills of Paphos, and the faun
Pipes in the noonday, and the nightingale sings on till
    dawn.

Nor failed they to obey her hest, and ere
The morning bee had stung the daffodil
With tiny fretful spear, or from its lair
The waking stag had leapt across the rill
And roused the ouzel, or the lizard crept
Athwart the sunny rock, beneath the grass their bodies
    slept.

And when day brake, within that silver shrine
Fed by the flames of cressets tremulous,
Queen Venus knelt and prayed to Proserpine
That she whose beauty made Death amorous
Should beg a guerdon from her pallid Lord,
And let Desire pass across dread Charon's icy ford.

III

In melancholy moonless Acheron,
Farm for the goodly earth and joyous day,
Where no spring ever buds, nor ripening sun
Weighs down the apple trees, nor flowery May
Chequers with chestnut blooms the grassy floor,
Where thrushes never sing, and piping linnets mate no
    more,

There by a dim and dark Lethæan well
Young Charmides was lying; wearily
He plucked the blossoms from the asphodel,
And with its little rifled treasury
Strewed the dull waters of the dusky stream,
And watched the white stars founder, and the land was
    like a dream,

When as he gazed into the watery glass
And through his brown hair's curly tangles scanned
His own wan face, a shadow seemed to pass
Across the mirror, and a little hand
Stole into his, and warm lips timidly
Brushed his pale cheeks, and breathed their secret forth
    into a sigh.

Then turned he round his weary eyes and saw,
And ever nigher still their faces came,
And nigher ever did their young mouths draw
Until they seemed one perfect rose of flame,
And longing arms around her neck he cast,
And felt her throbbing bosom, and his breath came hot
and fast,

And all his hoarded sweets were hers to kiss,
And all her maidenhood was his to slay,
And limb to limb in long and rapturous bliss
Their passion waxed and waned, – O why essay
To pipe again of love, too venturous reed!
Enough, enough that Eros laughed upon that flowerless
mead.

Too venturous poesy, O why essay
To pipe again of passion! fold thy wings
O'er daring Icarus and bid thy lay
Sleep hidden in the lyre's silent strings
Till thou hast found the old Castalian rill,
Or from the Lesbian waters plucked drowned Sappho's
golden quill!

Enough, enough that he whose life had been
A fiery pulse of sin, a splendid shame,
Could in the loveless land of Hades glean
One scorching harvest from those fields of flame
Where passion walks with naked unshod feet
And is not wounded, – ah! enough that once their lips
could meet

In that wild throb when all existences
Seemed narrowed to one single ecstasy
Which dies through its own sweetness and the stress
Of too much pleasure, ere Persephone
Had bade them serve her by the ebon throne
Of the pale God who in the fields of Enna loosed her
    zone.

Impressions

I Les Silhouettes

The sea is flecked with bars of
   grey,
The dull dead wind is out of tune,
And like a withered leaf the moon
Is blown across the stormy bay.

Etched clear upon the pallid sand
The black boat lies: a sailor boy
Clambers aboard in careless joy
With laughing face and gleaming
   hand.

And overhead the curlews cry,
Where through the dusky upland grass
The young brown-throated reapers pass,
Like silhouettes against the sky.

II La Fuite de la Lune

To outer senses there is peace,
A dreamy peace on either hand,
Deep silence in the shadowy land,
Deep silence where the shadows
   cease.

Save for a cry that echoes shrill
From some lone bird disconsolate;
A corncrake calling to its mate;
The answer from the misty hill.

And suddenly the moon withdraws
Her sickle from the lightening skies,
And to her sombre cavern flies,
Wrapped in a veil of yellow gauze.

The Grave of Keats

Rid of the world's injustice, and his pain,
He rests at last beneath God's veil of blue:
Taken from life when life and love were new
The youngest of the martyrs here is lain,
Fair as Sebastian, and as early slain.
No cypress shades his grave, no funeral yew,
But gentle violets weeping with the dew
Weave on his bones an ever-blossoming chain.
O proudest heart that broke for misery!
O sweetest lips since those of Mitylene!
O poet-painter of our English land!
Thy name was writ in water – it shall stand:
And tears like mine will keep thy memory green,
As Isabella did her Basil tree.

Theocritus

A Villanelle

O singer of Persephone!
In the dim meadows desolate
Dost thou remember Sicily?

Still through the ivy flits the bee
Where Amaryllis lies in state;
O Singer of Persephone!

Simætha calls on Hecate
And hears the wild dogs at the gate;
Dost thou remember Sicily?

Still by the light and laughing sea
Poor Polypheme bemoans his fate;
O Singer of Persephone!

And still in boyish rivalry
Young Daphnis challenges his mate;
Dost thou remember Sicily?

Slim Lacon keeps a goat for thee,
For thee the jocund shepherds wait;
O Singer of Persephone!
Dost thou remember Sicily?

In the Gold Room

A Harmony

Her ivory hands on the ivory keys
Strayed in a fitful fantasy,
Like the silver gleam when the poplar trees
Rustle their pale leaves listlessly,
Or the drifting foam of a restless sea
When the waves show their teeth in the flying breeze.

Her gold hair fell on the wall of gold
Like the delicate gossamer tangles spun
On the burnished disk of the marigold,
Or the sun-flower turning to meet the sun
When the gloom of the jealous night is done,
And the spear of the lily is aureoled.

And her sweet red lips on these lips of mine
Burned like the ruby fire set
In the swinging lamp of a crimson shrine,
Or the bleeding wounds of the pomegranate,
Or the heart of lotus drenched and wet
With the spilt-out blood of the rose-red wine.

Ballade de Marguerite

Normande

I am weary of lying within the chase
When the knights are meeting in market-place.

Nay, go not thou to the red-roofed town
Lest the hooves of the war-horse tread thee down.

But I would not go where the Squires ride,
I would only walk by my Lady's side.

Alack! and alack! thou art over bold,
A Forester's son may not eat off gold.

Will she love me the less that my Father is seen
Each Martinmas day in a doublet green?

Perchance she is sewing at tapestrie,
Spindle and loom are not meet for thee.

Ah, if she is working the arras bright
I might ravel the threads by the firelight.

Perchance she is hunting of the deer,
Flow could you follow o'er hill and mere?

Ah, if she is riding with the court,
I might run beside her and wind the morte.

Perchance she is kneeling in S. Denys,
(On her soul may our Lady have gramercy!)

Ah, if she is praying in lone chapelle,
I might swing the censer and ring the bell.

Come in my son, for you look sae pale,
Thy father shall fill thee a stoup of ale.

But who are these knights in bright array?
Is it a pageant the rich folks play?

'Tis the King of England from over sea,
Who has come unto visit our fair countrie.

But why does the curfew tool sae low
And why do the mourners walk a-row?

O 'tis Hugh of Amiens my sister's son
Who is lying stark, for his day is done.

Nay, nay, for I see white lilies clear,
It is no strong man who lies on the bier.

O 'tis old Dame Jeannette that kept the hall,
I knew she would die at the autumn fall.

Dame Jeannette had not that gold-brown hair,
Old Jeannette was not a maiden fair.

O 'tis none of our kith and none of our kin,
(Her soul may our Lady assoil from sin!)

But I hear the boy's voice chanting sweet,
'Elle est morte, la Marguerite.'

Come in my son and lie on the bed,
And let the dead folk bury their dead.

O mother, you know I loved her true:
O mother, hath one grave room for two?

The Dole of the King's Daughter

Breton

Seven stars in the still water,
And seven in the sky;
Seven sins on the King's daughter,
Deep in her soul to lie.

Red roses are at her feet,
(Roses are red in her red-gold hair,)
And O where her bosom and girdle meet
Red roses are hidden there.

Fair is the knight who lieth slain
Amid the rush and reed,
See the lean fishes that are fain
Upon dead men to feed.

Sweet is the page that lieth there,
(Cloth of gold is goodly prey,)
See the black ravens in the air,
Black, O black as the night are they.

What do they there so stark and dead?
(There is blood upon her hand)
Why are the lilies flecked with red,
(There is blood on the river sand.)

There are two that ride from the south and east,
And two from the north and west,

For the black raven a goodly feast,
For the King's daughter rest.

There is one man who loves her true
(Red, O red, is the stain of gore!)
He hath duggen a grave by the darksome yew,
(One grave will do for four.)

No moon in the still heaven,
In the black water none,
The sins on her soul are seven,
The sin upon his is one.

Amor Intellectualis

Oft have we trod the vales of Castaly
And heard sweet notes of sylvan music blown
From antique reeds to common folk unknown:
And often launched our bark upon that sea
Which the nine muses hold in empery,
And plowed free furrows through the wave and foam,
Nor spread reluctant sail for more safe home
Till we had freighted well our argosy.
Of which despoilèd treasures these remain,
Sordello's passion, and the honeyed line
Of young Endymion, lordly Tamburlaine
Driving him pampered jades, and more than these,
The seven-fold vision of the Florentine,
And grave-browed Milton's solemn harmonics.

Santa Decca

The Gods are dead: no longer do we bring
To gray-eyed Pallas crowns of olive-leaves!
Demeter's child no more hath tithe of sheaves,
And in the noon the careless shepherds sing,
For Pan is dead, and all the wantoning
By secret glade and devious haunt is o'er:
Young Hylas seeks the water-springs no more;
Great Pan is dead, and Mary's Son is King.

And yet – perchance in this sea-tranced isle,
Chewing the bitter fruit of memory,
Some God lies hidden in the asphodel.
Ah Love! if such there be then it were well
For us to fly his anger: nay, but see
The leaves are stirring: let us watch a-while.

A Vision

Two crowned Kings and One that stood alone
With no green weight of laurels round his head,
But with sad eyes as one uncomforted,
And wearied with man's never-ceasing moan
For sins no bleating victim can atone,
And sweet long lips with tears and kisses fed.
Girt was he in a garment black and red,
And at his feet I marked a broken stone
Which sent up lilies, dove-like, to his knees,
Now at their sight, my heart being lit with flame
I cried to Beatrice, 'Who are these?'
'Æschylos first, the second Sophokles,
And last (wide stream of tears!) Euripides.'

By the Arno

The oleander on the wall
Grows crimson in the dawning light,
Though the grey shadows of the night
Lie yet on Florence like a pall.

The dew is bright upon the hill,
And bright the blossoms overhead,
But ah! the grasshoppers have fled,
The little Attic song is still.

Only the leaves are gently stirred
By the soft breathing of the gale,
And in the almond-scented vale
The lonely nightingale is heard

The day will make thee silent soon,
O nightingale sing on for love!
While yet upon the shadowy grove
Splinter the arrows of the moon.

Before across the silent lawn
In sea-green mist the morning steals,
And to love's frightened eyes reveals
The long white fingers of the dawn.

Fast climbing up the eastern sky,
To grasp and slay the shuddering night,
All careless of my heart's delight,
Or if the nightingale should die.

Impression de Voyage

The sea was sapphire coloured, and the sky
Burned like a heated opal through the air;
We hoisted sail; the wind was blowing fair
For the blue lands that to the eastward lie.
From the steep prow I marked with quickening eye
Zakynthos, every olive grove and creek,
Ithaca's cliff, Lycaon's snowy peak,
And all the flower-strewn hills of Arcady.
The flapping of the sail against the mast,
The ripple of the water on the side,
The ripple of girls' laughter at the stern,
The only sounds: – when 'gan the West to burn,
And a red sun upon the seas to ride,
I stood upon the soil of Greece at last!

The Grave of Shelley

Like burnt-out torches by a sick man's bed
Gaunt cypress-trees stand round the sun-bleached stone;
Here doth the little night-owl make her throne,
And the slight lizard show his jewelled head.
And, where the chaliced poppies flame to red,
In the still chamber of yon pyramid
Surely some Old-World Sphinx lurks darkly hid,
Grim warder of this pleasaunce of the dead.

Ah! sweet indeed to rest within the womb
Of Earth great mother of eternal sleep,
But sweeter far for thee a restless tomb
In the blue cavern of an echoing deep,
Or where the tall ships founder in the gloom
Against the rocks of some wave-shattered steep.

Fabien dei Franchi

To My Friend Henry Irving

The silent room, the heavy creeping shade,
The dead that travel fast, the opening door,
The murdered brother rising through the floor,
The ghost's white fingers on thy shoulders laid,
And then the lonely duel in the glade,
The broken swords, the stifled scream, the gore,
Thy grand revengeful eyes when all is o'er, –
These things are well enough – but thou wert made
For more august creation! frenzied Lear
Should at thy bidding wander on the heath
With the shrill fool to mock him, Romeo
For thee should lure his love, and desperate fear
Pluck Richard's recreant dagger from its sheath –
Thou trumpet set for Shakespeare's lips to blow!

Phêdre

To Sarah Bernhardt

How vain and dull this common world must seem
To such a One as thou, who should'st have talked
At Florence with Mirandola, or walked
Through the cool olives of the Academe:
Thou should'st have gathered reeds from a green stream
For Goat-foot Pan's shrill piping, and have played
With the white girls in that Phæacian glade
Where grave Odysseus wakened from his dream.

Ah! surely once some urn of Attic clay
Held thy wan dust, and thou hast come again
Back to this common world so dull and vain,
For thou wert weary of the sunless day,
The heavy fields of scentless asphodel,
The loveless lips with which men kiss in Hell.

Camma

As one who poring on a Grecian urn
Scans the fair shapes some Attic hand hath made,
God with slim goddess, goodly man with maid,
And for their beauty's sake is loath to turn
And face the obvious day, must I not yearn
For many a secret moon of indolent bliss,
When is the midmost shrine of Artemis
I see thee standing, antique-limbed, and stern?

And yet – methinks I'd rather see thee play
That serpent of old Nile, whose witchery
Made Emperors drunken – come, great Egypt, shake
Our stage with all thy mimic pageants! Nay,
I am growing sick of unreal passions, make
The world thine Actium, me thine Antony!

Panthea

Nay, let us walk from fire unto fire,
From passionate pain to deadlier delight, –
I am too young to live without desire,
Too young art thou to waste this summer night
Asking those idle questions which of old
Man sought of seer and oracle, and no reply was told.

For sweet, to feel is better than to know,
And wisdom is a childless heritage,
One pulse of passion – youth's first fiery glow, –
Are worth the hoarded proverbs of the sage:
Vex not thy soul with dead philosophy,
Have we not lips to kiss with, hearts to love, and eyes to
    see!

Dost thou not hear the murmuring nightingale
Like water bubbling from a silver jar,
So soft she sings the envious moon is pale,
That high in heaven she hung so far
She cannot hear that love-enraptured tune, –
Mark how she wreathes each horn with mist, yon late
    and laboring moon.

White lilies, in whose cups the gold bees dream,
The fallen snow of petals where the breeze
Scatters the chestnut blossom, or the gleam
Of all our endless sins, our vain endeavour
Enough for thee, dost thou desire more?
Alas! the Gods will give naught else from their eternal
    store.

For our high Gods have sick and wearied grown
Of all our endless sins, our vain endeavour
For wasted days of youth to make atone
By pain or prayer or priest, and never, never,
Hearken they now to either good or ill,
But send their rain upon the just and the unjust at will.

They sit at ease, our Gods they sit at ease,
Strewing with leaves of rose their scented wine,
They sleep, they sleep, beneath the rocking trees
Where asphodel and yellow lotus twine,
Mourning the old glad days before they knew
What evil things the heart of man could dream, and
    dreaming do.

And far beneath the brazen floor, they see
Like swarming flies the crowd of little men,
The bustle of small lives, then wearily
Back to their lotus-haunts they turn again
Kissing each other's mouths, and mix more deep
The poppy-seeded draught which brings soft purple-
    lidded sleep.

There all day long the golden-vestured sun,
Their torch-bearer, stands with his torch a-blaze,
And when the gaudy web of noon is spun
By its twelve maidens through the crimson haze
Fresh from Endymion's arms comes forth the moon,
And the immortal Gods in toils of mortal passions swoon.

There walks Queen Juno through some dewy mead,
Her grand white feet flecked with the saffron dust

Of wind-stirred lilies, while young Ganymede
Leaps in the hot and amber-foaming must,
His curls all tossed, as when the eagle bare
The frightened boy from Ida through the blue Ionian air.

There in the green heart of some garden close
Queen Venus with the shepherd at her side,
Her warm soft body like the brier rose
Which would be white yet blushes at its pride,
Laughs low for love, till jealous Salmacis
Peers through the myrtle-leaves and sighs for pain of
    lonely bliss.

There never does that dreary northwind blow
Which leaves our English forests bleak and bare,
Nor ever falls the swift white-feathered snow,
Nor doth the red-toothed lightning ever dare
To wake them in the silver-fretted night
When we lie weeping for some sweet sad sin, some dead
    delight.

Alas! they know the far Lethæan spring,
The violet-hidden waters well they know,
Where one whose feet with tired wandering
Are faint and broken may take heart and go,
And from those dark depths cool and crystalline
Drink, and draw balm, and sleep for sleepless souls, and
    anodyne.

But we oppress our natures, God or Fate
Is our enemy, we starve and feed
On vain repentance – O we are born too late!

What balm for us in bruisèd poppy seed
Who crowd into one finite pulse of time
The joy of infinite love and the fierce pain of infinite
    crime.

O we are wearied of this sense of guilt,
Wearied of pleasures paramour despair,
Wearied of every temple we have built,
Wearied of every right, unanswered prayer,
For man is weak; God sleeps: and heaven is high:
One fiery-coloured moment: one great love: and lo! we
    die.

Ah! but no ferry-man with labouring pole
Nears his black shallop to the flowerless strand,
No little coin of bronze can bring the soul
Over Death's river to the sunless land,
Victim and wine and vow are all in vain,
The tomb is sealed; the soldiers watch; the dead rise not
    again.

We are resolved into the supreme air,
We are made one with what we touch and see,
With our heart's blood each crimson sun is fair,
With our young lives each spring-impassioned tree
Flames into green, the wildest beasts that range
The moor our kinsmen are, all life is one, and all is
    change.

With beat of systole and of diastole
One grand great light throbs through earth's giant heart,
And mighty waves of single Being roll

From nerve-less germ to man, for we are part
Of every rock and bird and beast and hill,
One with the things that prey on us, and one with what
    we kill.

From lower cells of waking life we pass
To full perfection; thus the world grows old:
We who are godlike now were once a mass
Of quivering purple flecked with bars of gold,
Unsentient or of joy or misery,
And tossed in terrible tangles of some wild and wind-
    swept sea.

This hot hard flame with which our bodies burn
Will make some meadow blaze with daffodil,
Ay! and those argent breasts of thine will turn
To water-lilies; the brown fields men till
Will be more fruitful for our love to-night,
Nothing is lost in nature, all things live in Death's
    despite.

The boy's first kiss, the hyacinth's first bell,
The man's last passion, and the last red spear
That from the lily leaps, the asphodel
Which will not let its blossoms blow for fear
Of too much beauty, and the timid shame
Of the young bridegroom at his lover's eyes – these with
    the same

One sacrament are consecrate, the earth
Not we alone hath passions hymeneal,
The yellow buttercups that shake for mirth

At daybreak know a pleasure not less real
Than we do, when in some fresh-blossoming wood
We draw the spring into our hearts, and feel that life is
   good.

So when men bury us beneath the yew
Thy crimson-stainèd mouth a rose will be,
And thy soft eyes lush bluebells dimmed with dew,
And when the white narcissus wantonly
Kisses the wind its playment, some faint joy
Will thrill our dust, and we will be again fond maid and
   boy.

And thus without life's conscious torturing pain
In some sweet flower we will feel the sun,
And from the linnet's throat will sing again,
And as two gorgeous-mailed snakes will run
Over our graves, or as two tigers creep
Through the hot jungle where the yellow-eyed huge lions
   sleep

And give them battle! How my heart leaps up
To think of that grand living after death
In beast and bird and flower, when this cup,
Being filled too full of spirit, bursts for breath,
And with the pale leaves of some autumn day
The soul earth's earliest conqueror becomes earth's last
   great prey.

O think of it! We shall inform ourselves
Into all sensuous life, the goat-foot Faun,
The Centaur, or the merry bright-eyed Elves

That leave their dancing rings to spite the dawn
Upon the meadows, shall not be more near
Than you and I to nature's mysteries, for we shall hear

The thrush's heart beat, and the daisies grow,
And the wan snowdrop sighing for the sun
On sunless days in winter, we shall know
By whom the silver gossamer is spun,
Who paints the diapered fritillaries,
On what wide wings from shivering pine to pine the
    eagle flies.

Ay! had we never loved at all, who knows
If yonder daffodil had lured the bee
Into its gilded womb, or any rose
Had hung with crimson lamps its little tree!
Methinks no leaf would ever bud in spring,
But for the lovers' lips that kiss, the poet's lips
    that sing.

Is the light vanished from our golden sun,
Or is this dædal-fashioned earth less fair,
That we are nature's heritors, and one
With every pulse of life that beats the air?
Rather new suns across the sky shall pass,
New splendour come unto the flower, new glory to the
    grass.

And we two lovers shall not sit afar,
Critics of nature, but the joyous sea
Shall be our raiment, and the bearded star
Shoot arrows at our pleasure! We shall be

Part of the mighty universal whole,
And through all æons mix and mingle with the Kosmic
  Soul!

We shall be notes in that great Symphony
Whose cadence circles through the rhythmic spheres,
And all the live World's throbbing heart shall be
One with our heart, the stealthy creeping years
Have lost their terrors now, we shall not die,
The Universe itself shall be our Immortality!

Impression: Le Reveillon

The sky is laced with fitful red,
The circling mists and shadows flee,
The dawn is rising from the sea,
Like a white lady from her bed.

And jagged brazen arrows fall
Athwart the feathers of the night,
And a long wave of yellow light
Breaks silently on tower and hall,

And spreading wide across the wold
Wakes into flight some fluttering bird,
And all the chestnut tops are stirred,
And all the branches streaked with gold.

At Verona

How steep the stairs within Kings' houses are
For exile-wearied feet as mine to tread,
And O how salt and bitter is the bread
Which falls from this Hound's table – better far
That I had died in the red ways of war,
Or that the gate of Florence bare my head,
Than to live thus, by all things comraded
Which seek the essence of my soul to mar.

'Curse God and die: what better hope than this?
He hath forgotten thee in all the bliss
Of his gold city, and eternal day' –
Nay peace: behind my prison's blinded bars
I do possess what none can take away,
My love, and all the glory of the stars.

Apologia

Is it thy will that I should wax and wane,
Barter my cloth of gold for hodden grey,
And at thy pleasure weave that web of pain
Whose brightest threads are each a wasted day?

Is it thy will – Love that I love so well –
That my Soul's House should be a tortured spot
Wherein, like evil paramours, must dwell
The quenchless flame, the worm that dieth not?

Nay, if it be thy will I shall endure,
And sell ambition at the common mart,
And let dull failure be my vestiture,
And sorrow dig its grave within my heart.

Perchance it may be better so – at least
I have not made my heart a heart of stone,
Nor starved my boyhood of its goodly feast,
Nor walked where Beauty is a thing unknown.

Many a man hath done so; sought to fence
In straitened bonds the soul that should be free,
Trodden the dusty road of common sense,
While all the forest sang of liberty,

Not marking how the spotted hawk in flight
Passed on wide pinion through the lofty air,
To where the steep untrodden mountain height
Caught the last tresses of the Sun God's hair.

Or how the little flower he trod upon,
The daisy, that white-feathered shield of gold,
Followed with wistful eyes the wandering sun
Content if once its leaves were aureoled.

But surely it is something to have been
The best beloved for a little while,
To have walked hand in hand with Love, and seen
His purple wings flit once across thy smile.

Ay! though the gorged asp of passion feed
On my boy's heart, yet have I burst the bars,
Stood face to face with Beauty, known indeed
The Love which moves the Sun and all the stars!

Quia Multum Amavi

Dear Heart, I think the young impassioned priest
When first he takes from out the hidden shrine
His God imprisoned in the Eucharist,
And eats the bread, and drinks the dreadful wine,

Feels not such awful wonder as I felt
When first my smitten eyes beat full on thee,
And all night long before thy feet I knelt
Till thou wert wearied of Idolatry.

Ah! had'st thou liked me less and loved me more,
Through all those summer days of joy and rain,
I had not now been sorrow's heritor,
Or stood a lackey in the House of Pain.

Yet, though remorse, youth's white-faced seneschal
Tread on my heels with all his retinue,
I am most glad I loved thee – think of all
The sums that go to make one speedwell blue!

Silentium Amoris

As oftentimes the too resplendent sun
Hurries the pallid and reluctant moon
Back to her sombre cave, ere she hath won
A single ballad from the nightingale,
So doth thy Beauty make my lips to fail,
And all my sweetest singing out of tune.

And as at dawn across the level mead
On wings impetuous some wind will come,
And with its too harsh kisses break the reed
Which was its only instrument of song,
So my too stormy passions work me wrong,
And for excess of Love my Love is dumb.

But surely unto Thee mine eyes did show
Why I am silent, and my lute unstrung;
Else it were better we should part, and go,
Thou to some lips of sweeter melody,
And I to nurse the barren memory
Of unkissed kisses, and songs never sung.

Her Voice

The wild bee reels from bough to bough
With his furry coat and his gauzy wing.
Now in a lily-cup, and now
Setting a jacinth bell a-swing,
In his wandering;
Sit closer love: it was here I trow
I made that vow,

Swore that two lives should be like one
As long as the sea-gull loved the sea,
As long as the sunflower sought the sun –
It shall be, I said, for eternity
'Twixt you and me!
Dear friend, those times are over and done,
Love's web is spun.

Look upward where the poplar trees
Sway and sway in the summer air,
Here in the valley never a breeze
Scatters the thistledowns, but there
Great winds blow fair
From the mighty murmuring mystical seas,
And the wave-lashed leas.

Look upward where the white gull screams
What does it see that we do not see?
Is that a star? or the lamp that gleams
On some outward voyaging argosy –
Ah! can it be
We have lived our lives in a land of dreams!
How sad it seems.

Sweet, there is nothing left to say
But this, that love is never lost.
Keen winter stabs the breasts of May
Whose crimson roses burst his frost,
Ships tempest-tossed
Will find a harbour in some bay,
And so we may.

And there is nothing left to do
But to kiss once again, and part,
Nay, there is nothing we should rue,
I have my beauty – you your Art.
Nay, do not start,
One world was not enough for two
Like me and you.

My Voice

Within this restless, hurried, modern world
We took our hearts' full pleasure – You and I,
And now the white sails of our ship are furled,
And spent the lading of our argosy.

Wherefore my cheeks before their time are wan,
For very weeping is my gladness fled
Sorrow hath paled my lip's vermilion,
And Ruin draws the curtains of my bed.

But all this crowded life has been to thee
No more than lyre, or lute, or subtle spell
Of viols, or the music of the sea
That sleeps, a mimic echo, in the shell.

Taedium Vitae

To stab my youth with desperate knife, to wear
This paltry age's gaudy livery,
To let each base hand filch my treasury,
To mesh my soul within a woman's hair,
And be mere Fortune's lackeyed groom – I swear,
I love it not! these things are less to me
Than the thin foam that frets upon the sea,
Less than the thistle-down of summer air
Which hath no seed: better to stand aloof
Far from these slanderous fools who mock my life
Knowing me not, better the lowliest roof
Fit for the meanest hind to sojourn in,
Than to go back to that hoarse cave of strife
Where my white soul first kissed the mouth of sin.

Humanitad

It is full winter now: the trees are bare,
Save where the cattle huddle from the cold
Beneath the pine, for it doth never wear
The Autumn's gaudy livery whose gold
Her jealous brother pilfers, but is true
To the green doublet; bitter is the wind, as though it blew

From Saturn's cave; a few thin wisps of hay
Lie on the sharp black hedges, where the wain
Dragged the sweet pillage of a summer's day
From the low meadows up the narrow lane;
Upon the half-thawed snow the bleating sheep
Press close against the hurdles, and the shivering
    housedogs creep

From the shut stable to the frozen stream
And back again disconsolate, and miss
The bawling shepherds and the noisy team;
And overhead in circling listlessness
The cawing rooks whirl round the frosted stack,
Or crowd the dripping boughs; and in the fen the
    ice-pools crack

Where the gaunt bittern stalks among the reeds
And flaps his wings, and stretches back his neck,
And hoots to see the moon; across the meads
Limps the poor frightened hare, a little speck;
And a stray seamew with its fretful cry
Flits like a sudden drift of snow against the dull grey sky.

Full winter: and a lusty goodman brings
His load of faggots from the chilly byre,
And stamps his feet upon the hearth, and flings
The sappy billets on the waning fire,
And laughs to see the sudden lightning scare
His children at their play; and yet, – the Spring is in the
     air,

Already the slim crocus stirs the snow,
And soon yon blanched fields will bloom again
With nodding cowslips for some lad to mow,
For with the first warm kisses of the rain
The winter's icy, sorrow breaks to tears,
And the brown thrushes mate, and with bright eyes the
     rabbit peers   ·

From the dark warren where the fir-cones lie,
And treads one snowdrop under foot and runs
Over the mossy knoll, and blackbirds fly
Across our path at evening, and the suns
Stay longer with us; ah! how good to see
Grass-girdled Spring in all her joy of laughing
     greenery

Dance through the hedges till the early rose,
(That sweet repentance of the thorny briar!)
Burst from its sheathèd emerald and disclose
The little quivering disk of golden fire
Which the bees know so well, for with it come
Pale boys love, sops-in-wine, and daffadillies all in
     bloom.

Then up and down the field the sower goes,
While close behind the laughing younker
    scares,
With shrilly whoop the black and thievish crows.
And then the chestnut-tree its glory wears,
And on the grass the creamy blossom falls
In odorous excess, and faint half-whispered madrigals

Steal from the bluebells' nodding carillons
Each breezy morn, and then white jessamine,
That star of its own heaven, snap-dragons
With lolling crimson tongues, and eglantine
In dusty velvets clad usurp the bed
And woodland empery, and when the lingering rose hath
    shed

Red leaf by leaf its folded panoply,
And pansies closed their purple-lidded eyes,
Chrysanthemums from gilded argosy
Unload their gaudy scentless merchandise
And violets getting overbold withdraw
From their shy nooks, and scarlet berries dot the leafless
    haw.

O happy field! and O thrice happy tree!
Soon will your queen in daisy-flowered smock,
And crown of flower-de-luce trip down the lea,
Soon will the lazy shepherds drive their flock
Back to the pasture by the pool, and soon
Through the green leaves will float the hum of
    murmuring bees at noon.

Soon will the glade be bright with bellamour,
The flower which wantons love, and those sweet nuns
Vale-lilies in their snowy vestiture
Will tell their bearded pearls, and carnations
With mitred dusky leaves will scent the wind,
And straggling traveller's joy each hedge with yellow stars
    will bind.

Dear Bride of Nature and most bounteous Spring!
That can'st give increase to the sweet-breath'd kine,
And to the kid its little horns, and bring
The soft and silky blossoms to the vine,
Where is that old nepenthe which of yore
Man got from poppy root and glossy-berried
    mandragore!

There was a time when any common bird
Could make me sing in unison, a time
When all the strings of boyish life were stirred
To quick response or more melodious rhyme
By every forest idyll; – do I change?
Or rather doth some evil thing through thy fair
    pleasaunce range?

Nay, nay, thou art the same: 'tis I who seek
To vex with sighs thy simple solitude,
And because fruitless tears bedew my cheek
Would have thee weep with me in brotherhood;
Fool! shall each wronged and restless spirit dare
To taint such wine with the salt poison of his own
    despair!

Thou art the same: 'tis I whose wretched soul
Takes discontent to be its paramour,
And gives its kingdom to the rude control
Of what should be its servitor – for sure
Wisdom is somewhere, though the stormy sea
Contain it not, and the huge deep answer ''Tis not in me.'

To burn with one clear flame, to stand erect
In natural honour, not to bend the knee
In profitless prostrations whose effect
Is by itself condemned, what alchemy
Can teach me this? what herb Medea brewed
Will bring the unexultant peace of essence not subdued?

The minor chord which ends the harmony,
And for its answering brother waits in vain,
Sobbing for incompleted melody
Dies a swan's death; but I the heir of pain
A silent Memnon with blank lidless eyes
Wait for the light and music of those suns which never
    rise.

The quanched-out torch, the lonely cypress-gloom,
The little dust stored in the narrow urn,
The gentle XAIPE of the Attic tomb, –
Were not these better far than to return
To my old fitful restless malady,
Or spend my days within the voiceless cave of misery?

Nay! for perchance that poppy-crownèd God
Is like the watcher by a sick man's bed
Who talks of sleep but gives it not; his rod

Hath lost its virtue, and, when all is said,
Death is too rude, too obvious a key
To solve one single secret in a life's philosophy.

And love! that noble madness, whose august
And inextinguishable might can slay
The soul with honeyed drugs — alas! I must
From such sweet ruin play the runaway,
Although too constant memory never can
Forget the arched splendor of those brows Olympian

Which for a little season made my youth
So soft a swoon of exquisite indolence
That all the chiding of more prudent Truth
Seemed the thin voice of jealousy — O Hence
Thou huntress deadlier than Artemis!
Go seek some other quarry! for of thy too perilous bliss

My lips have drunk enough — no more, no more —
Though Love himself should turn his gilded prow
Back to the troubled waters of this shore
Where I am wrecked and stranded, even now
The chariot wheels of passion sweep too near,
Hence! Hence! I pass unto a life more barren, more austere.

More barren — ay, those arms will never lean
Down through the trellised vines and draw my soul
In sweet reluctance through the tangled green;
Some other head must wear that aureole,
For I am Hers who loves not any man
Whose white and stainless bosom bears the sign
    Gorgonian.

Let Venus go and chuck her dainty page,
And kiss his mouth, and toss his curly hair,
With net and spear and hunting equipage
Let young Adonis to his tryst repair,
But me her fond and subtle-fashioned spell
Delights no more, though I could win her dearest citadel.

Ay, though I were that laughing shepherd boy
Who from Mount Ida saw the little cloud
Pass over Tenedos and lofty Troy
And knew the coming of the Queen, and bowed
In wonder at her feet, not for the sake
Of a new Helen would I bid her hand the apple take.

Then rise supreme Athena argent-limbed!
And, if my lips be musicless, inspire
At least my life: was not thy glory hymned
By one who gave to thee his sword and lyre
Like Æschylus at well-fought Marathon,
And died to show that Milton's England still could
    bear a son!

And yet I cannot tread the Portico
And live without desire, fear and pain,
Or nurture that wise calm which long ago
The grave Athenian master taught to men,
Self-poised, self-centered, and self-comforted,
To watch the world's vain phantasies go by with
    unbowed head.

Alas! that serene brow, those eloquent lips,
Those eyes that mirrored all eternity,

Rest in their own Colonos, an eclipse
Hath come on Wisdom, and Mnemosyne
Is childless; in the night which she had made
For lofty secure flight Athena's owl itself hath strayed.

Nor much with Science do I care to climb,
Although by strange and subtle witchery
She draw the moon from heaven: the Muse of Time
Unrolls her gorgeous-coloured tapestry
To no less eager eyes; often indeed
In the great epic of Polymnia's scroll I love to read

How Asia sent her myriad hosts to war
Against a little town, and panoplied
In gilded mail with jewelled scimetar,
White-shielded, purple-crested, rode the Mede
Between the waving poplars and the sea
Which men call Artemisium, till he saw Thermopylae

Its steep ravine spanned by a narrow wall,
And on the nearer side a little brood
Of careless lions holding festival!
And stood amazèd at such hardihood,
And pitched his tent upon the reedy shore,
And stayed two days to wonder, and then crept at
    midnight o'er

Some unfrequented height, and coming down
The autumn forests treacherously slew
What Sparta held most dear and was the crown
Of far Eurotas, and passed on, nor knew
How God had staked an evil net for him

In the small bay of Salamis – and yet, the page
    grows dim.

Its cadenced Greek delights me not, I feel
With such a goodly time too out of tune
To love it much: for like the Dial's wheel
That from its blinded darkness strikes the noon
Yet never sees the sun, so do my eyes
Restlessly follow that which from my cheated vision flies.

O for one grand unselfish simple life
To teach us what is Wisdom! speak ye hills
Of lone Helvellyn, for this note of strife
Shunned your untroubled crags and crystal rills,
Where is that Spirit which living blamelessly
Yet dared to kiss the smitten mouth of his own century!

Speak ye Rydalian laurels! where is He
Whose gentle head ye sheltered, that pure soul
Whose gracious days of uncrowned majesty
Through lowliest conduct touched the lofty goal
Where Love and Duty mingle! Him at least
The most high Laws were glad of, he had sat at
    Wisdom's feast,

But we are Learning's changelings, known by rote
The clarion watchword of each Grecian school
And follow none, the flawless sword which smote
The pagan Hydra is an effete tool
Which we ourselves have blunted, what man now
Shall scale the august ancient heights and to old Reverence
    bow?

One such indeed I saw, but, Ichabod!
Gone is that last dear son of Italy,
Who being man died for the sake of God,
And whose unrisen bones sleep peacefully.
O guard him, guard him well, my Giotto's tower,
Thou marble lily of the lily town! let not the lour

Of the rude tempest vex his slumber, or
The Arno with its tawny troubled gold
O'erleap its marge, no mightier conqueror
Clomb the high Capitol in the days of old
When Rome was indeed Rome, for Liberty
Walked like a Bride beside him, at which sight pale
    Mystery

Fled shrieking to her furthest somberest cell
With an old man who grabbled rusty keys,
Fled shuddering for that immemorial knell
With which oblivion buries dynasties
Swept like a wounded eagle on the blast,
As to the holy heart of Rome the great triumvir passed.

He knew the holiest heart and heights of Rome,
He drave the base wolf from the lion's lair,
And now lies dead by that empyreal dome
Which overtops Valdarno hung in air
By Brunelleschi – O Melpomene
Breathe through thy melancholy pipe thy sweetest
    threnody!

Breathe through the tragic stops such melodies
That Joy's self may grow jealous, and the Nine

Forget a-while their discreet emperies,
Mourning for him who on Rome's lordliest shrine
Lit for men's lives the light of Marathon,
And bare to sun-forgotten fields the fire of the sun!

O guard him, guard him well, my Giotto's tower,
Let some young Florentine each eventide
Bring coronals of that enchanted flower
Which the dim woods of Vallombrosa hide,
And deck the marble tomb wherein he lies
Whose soul is as some mighty orb unseen of mortal eyes.

Some mighty orb whose cycled wanderings,
Being tempest-driven to the furthest rim
Where Chaos meets Creation and the wings
Of the eternal chanting Cherubim
Are pavilioned on Nothing, passed away
Into a moonless void – and yet, though he is
    dust and clay,

He is not dead, the immemorial Fates
Forbid it, and the closing shears refrain,
Lift up your heads ye everlasting gates!
Ye argent clarions sound a loftier strain!
For the vile thing he hated lurks within
Its sombre house, alone with God and memories
    of sin.

Still what avails it that she sought her cave
That murderous mother of red harlotries?
At Munich on the marble architrave
The Grecian boys die smiling, but the seas

Which wash Ægina fret in loneliness
Not mirroring their beauty, so our lives grow colourless

For lack of our ideals, if one star
Flame torch-like in the heavens the unjust
Swift daylight kills it, and no trump of war
Can wake to passionate voice the silent dust
Which was Mazzini once! rich Niobe
For all her stony sorrows hath her sons, but Italy!

What Easter Day shall make her children rise,
Who were not Gods yet suffered, what sure feet
Shall find their graveclothes folded? what clear eyes
Shall see them bodily? O it were meet
To roll the stone from off the sepulchre
And kiss the bleeding roses of their wounds,
    in love of Her

Our Italy! our mother visible!
Most blessed among nations and most sad,
For whose dear sake the young Calabrian fell
That day at Aspromonte and was glad
That in an age when God was bought and sold
One man could die for Liberty! but we, burnt out
    and cold,

See Honour smitten on the cheek and gyves
Bind the sweet feet of Mercy: Poverty
Creeps through our sunless lanes and with sharp knives
Cuts the warm throats of children stealthily,
And no word said:– O we are wretched men
Unworthy of our great inheritance! where is the pen

Of austere Milton? where the mighty sword
Which slew its master righteously? the years
Have lost their ancient leader, and no word
Breaks from the voiceless tripod on our ears;
While as a ruined mother in some spasm
Bears a base child and loathes it, so our best
    enthusiasm

Genders unlawful children, Anarchy
Freedom's own Judas, the vile prodigal
License who steals the gold of Liberty
And yet nothing, Ignorance the real
One Fratricide since Cain, Envy the asp
That stings itself to anguish, Avarice whose
    palsied grasp

Is in its extent stiffened, moneyed Greed
For whose dull appetite men waste away
Amid the whirr of wheels and are the seed
Of things which slay their sower, these each day
Sees rife in England, and the gentle feet
Of Beauty tread no more the stones of each unlovely
    street.

What even Cromwell spared is desecrated
By weed and worm, left to the stormy play
Of wind and beating snow, or renovated
By more destructful hands: Time's worst decay
Will wreathe its ruins with some loveliness,
But these new Vandals can but make a rainproof
    barrenness.

Where is that Art which bade the Angels sing
Through Lincoln's lofty choir, till the air
Seems from such marble harmonies to ring
With sweeter song than common lips can dare
To draw from actual reed? ah! where is now
The cunning hand which made the flowering hawthorn
    branches bow

For Southwell's arch, and carved the House of One
Who loved the lilies of the field with all
Our dearest English flowers? the same sun
Rises for us: the seasons natural
Weave the same tapestry of green and gray:
The unchanged hills are with us: but that Spirit hath
    passed away.

And yet perchance it may be better so,
For Tyranny is an incestuous Queen,
Murder her brother is her bedfellow,
And the Plague chambers with her: in obscene
And bloody paths her treacherous feet are set;
Better the empty desert and a soul inviolate!

For gentle brotherhood, the harmony
Of living in the healthful air, the swift
Clean beauty of strong limbs when men are free
And women chaste, these are the things which lift
Our souls up more than even Agnolo's
Gaunt blinded Sibyl poring o'er the scroll of human woes,

Or Titian's little maiden on the stair
White as her own sweet lily and as tall,

Or Mona Lisa smiling through her hair, –
Ah! somehow life is bigger after all
Than any painted angel could we see
The God that is within us! The old Greek serenity

Which curbs the passion of that level line
Of marble youths, who with untroubled eyes
And chastened limbs ride round Athena's shrine
And mirror her divine economies,
And balanced symmetry of what in man
Would else wage ceaseless warfare – this at least within
    the span

Between our mother's kisses and the grave
Might so inform our lives, that we could win
Such mighty empires that from her cave
Temptation would grow hoarse, and pallid Sin
Would walk ashamed of his adulteries,
And Passion creep from out the House of Lust with
    startled eyes.

To make the Body and the Spirit one
With all right things, till no thing live in vain
From morn to noon, but in sweet unison
With every pulse of flesh and throb of pain
The Soul in flawless essence high enthroned,
Against all outer vain attack invincibly bastioned,

Mark with serene impartiality
The strife of things, and yet be comforted,
Knowing that by the chain causality
All separate existences are wed

Into one supreme whole, whose utterance
Is joy, or holier praise! ah! surely this were governance

Of life in most august omnipresence,
Through which the rational intellect would find
In passion its expression, and mere sense
Ignoble else, lend fire to the mind,
And being joined with it in harmony
More mystical than that which binds the stars planetary,

Strike from their several tones one octave chord
Whose cadence being measureless would fly
Through all the circling spheres, then to its Lord
Return refreshed with its new empery
And more exultant power – this indeed
Could we but reach it were to find the last, the perfect creed.

Ah! it was easy when the world was young
To keep one's life free and inviolate,
From our sad lips another song is rung,
By our own hands our heads are desecrate,
Wanderers in drear exile and dispossessed
Of what should be our own, we can but feed on wild
    unrest.

Somehow the grace, the bloom of things has flown,
And of all men we are most wretched who
Must live each other's lives and not our own
For very pity's sake and then undo
All that we live for – it was otherwise
When soul and body seemed to blend in mystic symphonies.

But we have left those gentle haunts to pass
With weary feet to the new Calvary,
Where we behold, as one who in a glass
Sees his own face, self-slain Humanity,
And in the dumb reproach of that sad gaze
Learn what an awful phantom the red hand of
    man can raise.

O smitten mouth! O forehead crowned with thorn!
O chalice of all common miseries!
Thou for our sakes that loved thee not hast borne
An agony of endless centuries,
And we were vain and ignorant nor knew
That when we stabbed thy heart it was our own real
    hearts we slew.

Being ourselves the sowers and the seeds,
The night that covers and the lights that fade,
The spear that pierces and the side that bleeds,
The lips betraying and the life betrayed;
The deep hath calm: the moon hath rest: but we
Lords of the natural world are yet our own dread
    enemy.

Is this the end of all that primal force
Which, in its changes being still the same,
From eyeless Chaos cleft its upward course,
Through ravenous seas and whirling rocks and flame,
Till the suns met in heaven and began
Their cycles, and the morning stars sang, and the
    Word was Man!

Nay, nay, we are but crucified, and though
The bloody sweat falls from our brows like rain,
Loosen the nails – we shall come down I know,
Stanch the red wounds – we shall be whole again,
No need have we of hyssop-laden rod,
That which is purely human that is Godlike, that is God.

From Spring Days to Winter

In the glad springtime when leaves were green,
O merrily the throstle sings!
I sought, amid the tangled sheen,
Love whom mine eyes had never seen,
O the glad dove has golden wings!

Between the blossoms red and white,
O merrily the throstle sings!
My love first came into my sight,
O perfect vision of delight,
O the glad dove has golden wings!

The yellow apples glowed like fire.
O merrily the throstle sings!
O Love too great for lip or lyre,
Blown rose of love and of desire,
O the glad dove has golden wings!

But now with snow the tree is grey,
Ah, sadly now the throstle sings!
My love is dead: ah! well-a-day,
See at her silent feet I lay
A dove with broken wings!
Ah, Love! ah, Love! that thou wert slain –
Fond Dove, fond Dove return again!

The True Knowledge

Thou knowest all; I seek in vain
What lands to till or sow with seed —
The land is black with briar and weed,
Nor cares for falling tears or rain.

Thou knowest all; I sit and wait
With blinded eyes and hands that fail,
Till the last lifting of the veil
And the first opening of the gate.

Thou knowest all; I cannot see.
I trust I shall not live in vain,
I know that we shall meet again
In some divine eternity.

Under the Balcony

O beautiful star with the crimson mouth!
O moon with the brows of gold!
Rise up, rise up, from the odorous south!
And light for my love her way,
Lest her little feet should stray
On the windy hill and the wold!
O beautiful star with the crimson mouth!
O moon with the brows of gold!

O ship that shakes on the desolate sea!
O ship with the wet, white sail!
Put in, put in, to the port to me!
For my love and I would go
To the land where the daffodils blow
In the heart of a violet dale!
O ship that shakes on the desolate sea!
O ship with the wet, white sail!

O rapturous bird with the low, sweet note!
O bird that sits on the spray!
Sing on, sing on, from your soft brown throat!
And my love in her little bed
Will listen, and lift her head
From the pillow, and come my way!
O rapturous bird with the low, sweet note!
O bird that sits on the spray!

O blossom that hangs in the tremulous air!
O blossom with lips of snow!
Come down, come down, for my love to wear!

You will die on her head in a crown,
You will die in a fold of her gown,
To her little light heart you will go!
O blossom that hangs in the tremulous air!
O blossom with lips of snow!

The Harlot's House

We caught the tread of dancing feet,
We loitered down the moonlit street,
And stopped beneath the harlot's house.

Inside, above the din and fray,
We heard the loud musicians play
The 'Treues Liebes Herz' of Strauss.

Like strange mechanical grotesques,
Making fantastic arabesques,
The shadows raced across the blind.

We watched the ghostly dancers spin
To sound of horn and violin,
Like black leaves wheeling in the wind.

Like wire-pulled automatons,
Slim silhouetted skeletons
Went sidling through the slow quadrille,

Then took each other by the hand,
And danced a stately saraband;
Their laughter echoed thin and shrill.

Sometimes a clockwork puppet pressed
A phantom lover to her breast,
Sometimes they seemed to try to sing.

Sometimes a horrible marionette
Came out, and smoked its cigarette
Upon the steps like a live thing.

Then, turning to my love, I said,
'The dead are dancing with the dead,
The dust is whirling with the dust.'

But she – she heard the violin,
And left my side, and entered in:
Love passed into the house of lust.

Then suddenly the tune went false,
The dancers wearied of the waltz,
The shadows ceased to wheel and whirl.

And down the long and silent street,
The dawn, with silver-sandalled feet,
Crept like a frightened girl.

Le Jardin des Tuileries

This winter air is keen and cold,
And keen and cold this winter sun,
But round my chair the children run
Like little things of dancing gold.

Sometimes about the painted kiosk
The mimic soldiers strut and stride,
Sometimes the blue-eyed brigands hide
In the bleak tangles of the bosk.

And sometimes, while the old nurse cons
Her book, they steal across the square,
And launch their paper navies where
Huge Triton writhes in greenish bronze.

And now in mimic flight they flee,
And now they rush, a boisterous band –
And, tiny hand on tiny hand,
Climb up the black and leafless tree.

Ah! cruel tree! if I were you,
And children climbed me, for their sake
Though it be winter I would break
Into spring blossoms white and blue!

On the Sale by Auction of Keats' Love Letters

These are the letters which Endymion wrote
To one he loved in secret, and apart.
And now the brawlers of the auction mart
Bargain and bid for each poor blotted note,
Ay! for each separate pulse of passion quote
The merchant's price. I think they love not art
Who break the crystal of a poet's heart
That small and sickly eyes may glare and gloat.
Is it not said that many years ago,
In a far Eastern town, some soldiers ran
With torches through the midnight, and began
To wrangle for mean raiment, and to throw
Dice for the garments of a wretched man,
Not knowing the God's wonder, or His woe?

The New Remorse

The sin was mine; I did not understand.
So now is music prisoned in her cave,
Save where some ebbing desultory wave
Frets with its restless whirls this meagre strand.
And in the withered hollow of this land
Hath Summer dug herself so deep a grave,
That hardly can the leaden willow crave
One silver blossom from keen Winter's hand.

But who is this who cometh by the shore?
(Nay, love, look up and wonder!) Who is this
Who cometh in dyed garments from the South?
It is thy new-found Lord, and he shall kiss
The yet unravished roses of thy mouth,
And I shall weep and worship, as before.

Canzonet

I have no store
Of gryphon-guarded gold;
Now, as before,
Bare is the shepherd's fold.
Rubies nor pearls
Have I to gem thy throat;
Yet woodland girls
Have loved the shepherd's note.

Then pluck a reed
And bid me sing to thee,
For I would feed
Thine ears with melody,
Who art more fair
Than fairest fleur-de-lys,
More sweet and rare
Than sweetest ambergris.

What dost thou fear?
Young Hyacinth is slain,
Pan is not here,
And will not come again.
No horned Faun
Treads down the yellow leas,
No God at dawn
Steals through the olive trees.

Hylas is dead,
Nor will he e'er divine
Those little red

Rose-petalled lips of thine.
On the high hill
No ivory dryads play,
Silver and still
Sinks the sad autumn day.

In the Forest

Out of the mid-wood's twilight
Into the meadow's dawn,
Ivory limbed and brown-eyed,
Flashes my Faun!

He skips through the copses singing,
And his shadow dances along,
And I know not which I should follow,
Shadow or song!

O Hunter, snare me his shadow!
O Nightingale, catch me his strain!
Else moonstruck with music and madness
I track him in vain!

To My Wife

With a Copy of My Poems

I can write no stately proem
As a prelude to my lay;
From a poet to a poem
I would dare to say.

For if of these fallen petals
One to you seem fair,
Love will waft it till it settles
On your hair.

And when wind and winter harden
All the loveless land,
It will whisper of the garden,
You will understand.

Roses and Rue

With a Copy of 'A House of Pomegranates'
(To L. L.)

Could we dig up this long-buried
   treasure,
Were it worth the pleasure,
We never could learn love's song,
We are parted too long.

Could the passionate past that is fled
Call back its dead,
Could we live it all over again,
Were it worth the pain!

I remember we used to meet
By an ivied seat,
And you warbled each pretty word
With the air of a bird;

And your voice had a quaver in it,
Just like a linnet,
And shook, as the blackbird's throat
With its last big note;

And your eyes, they were green and grey
Like an April day,
But lit into amethyst
When I stooped and kissed;

And your mouth, it would never smile
For a long, long while,
Then it rippled all over with laughter
Five minutes after.

You were always afraid of a shower,
Just like a flower:
I remember you started and ran
When the rain began.

I remember I never could catch you,
For no one could match you,
You had wonderful, luminous, fleet,
Little wings to your feet.

I remember your hair – did I tie it?
For it always ran riot –
Like a tangled sunbeam of gold:
These things are old.

I remember so well the room,
And the lilac bloom
That beat at the dripping pane
In the warm June rain;

And the colour of your gown,
It was amber-brown,
And two yellow satin bows
From your shoulders rose.

And the handkerchief of French lace
Which you held to your face –

Had a small tear left a stain?
Or was it the rain?

On your hand as it waved adieu
There were veins of blue;
In your voice as it said good-bye
Was a petulant cry,

'You have only wasted your life.'
(Ah, that was the knife!)
When I rushed through the garden gate
It was all too late.

Could we live it over again,
Were it worth the pain,
Could the passionate past that is fled
Call back its dead!

Well, if my heart must break,
Dear love, for your sake,
It will break in music, I know,
Poets' hearts break so.

But strange that I was not told
That the brain can hold
In a tiny ivory cell
God's heaven and hell.

Desespoir

The seasons send their ruin as they go,
For in the spring the narciss shows its head
Nor withers till the rose has flamed to red,
And in the autumn purple violets blow,
And the slim crocus stirs the winter snow;
Wherefore yon leafless trees will bloom again
And this grey land grow green with summer rain
And send up cowslips for some boy to mow.

But what of life whose bitter hungry sea
Flows at our heels, and gloom of sunless night
Covers the days which never more return?
Ambition, love and all the thoughts that burn
We lose too soon, and only find delight
In withered husks of some dead memory.

Pan

I

O goat-foot God of Arcady!
This modern world is grey and old,
And what remains to us of thee?

No more the shepherd lads in glee
Throw apples at thy wattled fold,
O goat-foot God of Arcady!

Nor through the laurels can one see
Thy soft brown limbs, thy beard of gold,
And what remains to us of thee?

And dull and dead our Thames would be,
For here the winds are chill and cold,
O goat-foot God of Arcady!

Then keep the tomb of Helice,
Thine olive-woods, thy vine-clad wold,
And what remains to us of thee?

Though many an unsung elegy
Sleeps in the reeds our rivers hold,
O goat-foot God of Arcady!
Ah, what remains to us of thee?

II

Ah, leave the hills of Arcady,
Thy satyrs and their wanton play,
This modern world hath need of thee.

No nymph of Faun indeed have we,
For Faun and nymph are old and grey,
Ah, leave the hills of Arcady!

This is the land where liberty
Lit grave-browed Milton on his way,
This modern world hath need of thee!

A land of ancient chivalry
Where gentle Sidney saw the day,
Ah, leave the hills of Arcady.

This fierce sea-lion of the sea,
This England lacks some stronger lay,
This modern world hath need of thee!

Then blow some trumpet loud and free,
And give thine oaten pipe away,
Ah, leave the hills of Arcady!
This modern world hath need of thee!

The Sphinx

In a dim corner of my room for longer than my fancy
   thinks
A beautiful and silent Sphinx has watched me through the
   shifting gloom.

Inviolate and immobile she does not rise she does not stir
For silver moons are naught to her and naught to her the
   suns that reel.

Red follows grey across the air, the waves of moonlight
   ebb and flow
But with the Dawn she does not go and in the night-time
   she is there.

Dawn follows Dawn and Nights grow old and all the
   while this curious cat
Lies couching on the Chinese mat with eyes of satin
   rimmed with gold.

Upon the mat she lies and leers and on the tawny throat
   of her
Flutters the soft and silky fur or ripples to her pointed ears.

Come forth, my lovely seneschal! so somnolent, so
   statuesque!
Come forth you exquisite grotesque! half woman and half
   animal!

Come forth my lovely languorous Sphinx! and put your
   head upon my knee!

And let me stroke your throat and see your body spotted
  like the Lynx!

And let me touch those curving claws of yellow ivory and
  grasp
The tail that like a monstrous Asp coils round your heavy
  velvet paws!

A thousand weary centuries are thine while I have hardly
  seen
Some twenty summers cast their green for Autumn's
  gaudy liveries.

But you can read the Hieroglyphs on the great sandstone
  obelisks,
And you have talked with Basilisks, and you have looked
  on Hippogriffs.

O tell me, were you standing by when Isis to Osiris
  knelt?
And did you watch the Egyptian melt her union for
  Antony

And drink the jewel-drunken wine and bend her head in
  mimic awe
To see the huge proconsul draw the salted tunny from the
  brine?

And did you mark the Cyprian kiss white Adon on his
  catafalque?
And did you follow Amenalk, the God of Heliopolis?

And did you talk with Thoth, and did you hear the
    moon-horned Io weep?
And know the painted kings who sleep beneath the
    wedge-shaped Pyramid?

Lift up your large black satin eyes which are like cushions
    where one sinks!
Fawn at my feet, fantastic Sphinx! and sing me all your
    memories!

Sing to me of the Jewish maid who wandered with the
    Holy Child,
And how you led them through the wild, and how they
    slept beneath your shade.

Sing to me of that odorous green eve when crouching by
    the marge
You heard from Adrian's gilded barge the laughter of
    Antinous

And lapped the stream and fed your drouth and watched
    with hot and hungry stare
The ivory body of that rare young slave with his
    pomegranate mouth!

Sing to me of the Labyrinth in which the twi-formed bull
    was stalled!
Sing to me of the night you crawled across the temple's
    granite plinth

When through the purple corridors the screaming scarlet
    Ibis flew

In terror, and a horrid dew dripped from the moaning
    Mandragores,

And the great torpid crocodile within the tank shed slimy
    tears,
And tare the jewels from his ears and staggered back into
    the Nile,

And the priests cursed you with shrill psalms as in your
    claws you seized their snake
And crept away with it to slake your passion by the
    shuddering palms.

Who were your lovers? who were they who wrestled for
    you in the dust?
Which was the vessel of your Lust? What Leman had
    you, every day?

Did giant Lizards come and crouch before you on the
    reedy banks?
Did Gryphons with great metal flanks leap on you in your
    trampled couch?

Did monstrous hippopotami come sidling toward you in
    the mist?
Did gilt-scaled dragons writhe and twist with passion as
    you passed them by?

And from the brick-built Lycian tomb what horrible
    Chimera came
With fearful heads and fearful flame to breed new
    wonders from your womb?

Or had you shameful secret quests and did you harry to
  your home
Some Nereid coiled in amber foam with curious rock
  crystal breasts?

Or did you treading through the froth call to the brown
  Sidonian
For tidings of Leviathan, Leviathan or Behemoth?

Or did you when the sun was set climb up the cactus-
  covered slope
To meet your swarthy Ethiop whose body was of
  polished jet?

Or did you while the earthen skiffs dropped down the
  grey Nilotic flats
At twilight and the flickering bats flew round the temple's
  triple glyphs

Steal to the border of the bar and swim across the silent
  lake
And slink into the vault and make the Pyramid your lúpanar

Till from each black sarcophagus rose up the painted
  swathèd dead?
Or did you lure unto your bed the ivory-horned
  Tragelaphos?

Or did you love the god of flies who plagued the
  Hebrews and was splashed
With wine unto the waist? or Pasht, who had green
  beryls for her eyes?

Or that young god, the Tyrian, who was more amorous
    than the dove
Of Ashtaroth? or did you love the god of the
    Assyrian

Whose wings, like strange transparent talc, rose high
    above his hawk-faced head,
Painted with silver and with red and ribbed with rods of
    Oreichalch?

Or did huge Apis from his car leap down and lay before
    your feet
Big blossoms of the honey-sweet and honey-coloured
    nenuphar?

How subtle-secret is your smile! Did you love none
    then? Nay, I know
Great Ammon was your bedfellow! He lay with you
    beside the Nile!

The river-horses in the slime trumpeted when they saw
    him come
Odorous with Syrian galbanum and smeared with
    spikenard and with thyme.

He came along the river bank like some tall galley
    argent-sailed,
He strode across the waters, mailed in beauty, and the
    waters sank.

He strode across the desert sand: he reached the valley
    where you lay:

He waited till the dawn of day: then touched your black
    breasts with his hand.

You kissed his mouth with mouths of flame: you made
    the hornèd god your own:
You stood behind him on his throne: you called him by
    his secret name.

You whispered monstrous oracles into the caverns of his
    ears:
With blood of goats and blood of steers you taught him
    monstrous miracles.

White Ammon was your bedfellow! Your chamber was
    the steaming Nile!
And with your curved archaic smile you watched his
    passion come and go.

With Syrian oils his brows were bright: and wide-spread
    as a tent at noon
His marble limbs made pale the moon and lent the day a
    larger light.

His long hair was nine cubits' span and coloured like that
    yellow gem
Which hidden in their garment's hem the merchants
    bring from Kurdistan.

His face was as the must that lies upon a vat of
    new-made wine:
The seas could not insapphirine the perfect azure of his
    eyes.

His thick soft throat was white as milk and threaded with
    thin veins of blue:
And curious pearls like frozen dew were broidered on his
    flowing silk.

On pearl and porphyry pedestalled he was too bright to
    look upon:
For on his ivory breast there shone the wondrous ocean-
    emerald,

That mystic moonlit jewel which some diver of the
    Colchian caves
Had found beneath the blackening waves and carried to
    the Colchian witch.

Before his gilded galiot ran naked vine-wreathed
    corybants,
And lines of swaying elephants knelt down to draw his
    chariot,

And lines of swarthy Nubians bare up his litter as he
    rode
Down the great granite-paven road between the nodding
    peacock-fans.

The merchants brought him steatite from Sidon in their
    painted ships:
The meanest cup that touched his lips was fashioned from
    a chrysolite.

The merchants brought him cedar chests of rich apparel
    bound with cords:

His train was borne by Memphian lords: young kings
    were glad to be his guests.

Ten hundred shaven priests did bow to Ammon's altar day
    and night,
Ten hundred lamps did wave their light through Ammon's
    carven house – and now

Foul snake and speckled adder with their young ones
    crawl from stone to stone
For ruined is the house and prone the great rose-marble
    monolith!

Wild ass or trotting jackal comes and couches in the
    mouldering gates:
Wild satyrs call unto their mates across the fallen fluted
    drums.

And on the summit of the pile the blue-faced ape of
    Horus sits
And gibbers while the fig-tree splits the pillars of the
    peristyle

The god is scattered here and there: deep hidden in the
    windy sand
I saw his giant granite hand still clenched in impotent
    despair.

And many a wandering caravan of stately negroes silken-
    shawled,
Crossing the desert, halts appalled before the neck that
    none can span.

And many a bearded Bedouin draws back his yellow-
    striped burnous
To gaze upon the Titan thews of him who was thy
    paladin.

Go, seek his fragments on the moor and wash them in
    the evening dew,
And from their pieces make anew thy mutilated
    paramour!

Go, seek them where they lie alone and from their broken
    pieces make
Thy bruisèd bedfellow! And wake mad passions in the
    senseless stone!

Charm his dull ear with Syrian hymns! he loved your
    body! oh, be kind,
Pour spikenard on his hair, and wind soft rolls of linen
    round his limbs!

Wind round his head the figured coins! stain with red
    fruits those pallid lips!
Weave purple for his shrunken hips! and purple for his
    barren loins!

Away to Egypt! Have no fear. Only one God has ever
    died.
Only one God has let His side be wounded by a soldier's
    spear.

But these, thy lovers, are not dead. Still by the hundred-
    cubit gate

Dog-faced Anubis sits in state with lotus-lilies for thy
head.

Still from his chair of porphyry gaunt Memnon strains his
lidless eyes
Across the empty land, and cries each yellow morning
unto thee.

And Nilus with his broken horn lies in his black and
oozy bed
And till thy coming will not spread his waters on the
withering corn.

Your lovers are not dead, I know. They will rise up and
hear your voice
And clash their cymbals and rejoice and run to kiss your
mouth! And so,

Set wings upon your argosies! Set horses to your ebon
car!
Back to your Nile! Or if you are grown sick of dead
divinities

Follow some roving lion's spoor across the copper-
coloured plain,
Reach out and hale him by the mane and bid him be
your paramour!

Couch by his side upon the grass and set your white
teeth in his throat
And when you hear his dying note lash your long flanks
of polished brass

And take a tiger for your mate, whose amber sides are
    flecked with black,
And ride upon his gilded back in triumph through the
    Theban gate,

And toy with him in amorous jests, and when he turns,
    and snarls, and gnaws,
O smite him with your jasper claws! and bruise him with
    your agate breasts!

Why are you tarrying? Get hence! I weary of your
    sullen ways,
I weary of your steadfast gaze, your somnolent
    magnificence.

Your horrible and heavy breath makes the light flicker in
    the lamp,
And on my brow I feel the damp and dreadful dews of
    night and death.

Your eyes are like fantastic moons that shiver in some
    stagnant lake,
Your tongue is like a scarlet snake that dances to fantastic
    tunes,

Your pulse makes poisonous melodies, and your black
    throat is like the hole
Left by some torch or burning coal on Saracenic
    tapestries.

Away! The sulphur-coloured stars are hurrying through
    the Western gate!

Away! Or it may be too late to climb their silent silver
    cars!

See, the dawn shivers round the grey gilt-dialled towers,
    and the rain
Streams down each diamonded pane and blurs with tears
    the wannish day.

What snake-tressed fury fresh from Hell, with uncouth
    gestures and unclean,
Stole from the poppy-drowsy queen and led you to a
    student's cell?

What songless tongueless ghost of sin crept through the
    curtains of the night,
And saw my taper burning bright, and knocked, and bade
    you enter in?

Are there not others more accursed, whiter with leprosies
    than I?
Are Abana and Pharphar dry that you come here to slake
    your thirst?

Get hence, you loathsome mystery! Hideous animal, get
    hence!
You wake in me each bestial sense, you make me what I
    would not be.

You make my creed a barren sham, you wake foul dreams
    of sensual life,
And Atys with his blood-stained knife were better than
    the thing I am.

False Sphinx! False Sphinx! By reedy Styx old Charon,
    leaning on his oar,
Waits for my coin. Go thou before, and leave me to my
    crucifix,

Whose pallid burden, sick with pain, watches the world
    with wearied eyes,
And weeps for every soul that dies, and weeps for every
    soul in vain.

The Ballad of Reading Gaol

I

He did not wear his scarlet coat,
For blood and wine are red,
And blood and wine were on his hands
When they found him with the dead,
The poor dead woman whom he loved,
And murdered in her bed.

He walked amongst the Trial Men
In a suit of shabby grey;
A cricket cap was on his head,
And his step seemed light and gay;
But I never saw a man who looked
So wistfully at the day.

I never saw a man who looked
With such a wistful eye
Upon that little tent of blue
Which prisoners call the sky,
And at every drifting cloud that went
With sails of silver by.

I walked, with other souls in pain,
Within another ring,
And was wondering if the man had done
A great or little thing,
When a voice behind me whispered low,
'That fellow's got to swing.'

Dear Christ! the very prison walls
Suddenly seemed to reel,
And the sky above my head became
Like a casque of scorching steel;
And, though I was a soul in pain,
My pain I could not feel.

I only knew what hunted thought
Quickened his step, and why
He looked upon the garish day
With such a wistful eye;
The man had killed the thing he loved,
And so he had to die.

Yet each man kills the thing he loves,
By each let this be heard,
Some do it with a bitter look,
Some with a flattering word,
The coward does it with a kiss,
The brave man with a sword!

Some kill their love when they are young,
And some when they are old;
Some strangle with the hands of Lust,
Some with the hands of Gold:
The kindest use a knife, because
The dead so soon grow cold.

Some love too little, some too long,
Some sell, and others buy;
Some do the deed with many tears,
And some without a sigh:

For each man kills the thing he loves,
Yet each man does not die.

He does not die a death of shame
On a day of dark disgrace,
Nor have a noose about his neck,
Nor a cloth upon his face,
Nor drop feet foremost through the floor
Into an empty space.

He does not sit with silent men
Who watch him night and day;
Who watch him when he tries to weep,
And when he tries to pray;
Who watch him lest himself should rob
The prison of its prey.

He does not wake at dawn to see
Dread figures throng his room,
The shivering Chaplain robed in white,
The Sheriff stern with gloom,
And the Governor all in shiny black,
With the yellow face of Doom.

He does not rise in piteous haste
To put on convict-clothes,
While some coarse-mouthed Doctor gloats,
    and notes
Each new and nerve-twitched pose,
Fingering a watch whose little ticks
Are like horrible hammer-blows.

He does not know that sickening thirst
That sands one's throat, before
The hangman with his gardener's gloves
Slips through the padded door,
And binds one with three leathern thongs,
That the throat may thirst no more.

He does not bend his head to hear
The Burial Office read,
Nor, while the terror of his soul
Tells him he is not dead,
Cross his own coffin, as he moves
Into the hideous shed.

He does not stare upon the air
Through a little roof of glass:
He does not pray with lips of clay
For his agony to pass;
Nor feel upon his shuddering cheek
The kiss of Caiaphas.

II

Six weeks our guardsman walked the yard,
In the suit of shabby grey:
His cricket cap was on his head,
And his step seemed light and gay,
But I never saw a man who looked
So wistfully at the day.

I never saw a man who looked
With such a wistful eye
Upon that little tent of blue

Which prisoners call the sky,
And at every wandering cloud that trailed
Its ravelled fleeces by.

He did not wring his hands, as do
Those witless men who dare
To try to rear the changeling Hope
In the cave of black Despair:
He only looked upon the sun,
And drank the morning air.

He did not wring his hands nor weep,
Nor did he peek or pine,
But he drank the air as though it held
Some healthful anodyne;
With open mouth he drank the sun
As though it had been wine!

And I and all the souls in pain,
Who tramped the other ring,
Forgot if we ourselves had done
A great or little thing,
And watched with gaze of dull amaze
The man who had to swing.

And strange it was to see him pass
With a step so light and gay,
And strange it was to see him look
So wistfully at the day,
And strange it was to think that he
Had such a debt to pay.

For oak and elm have pleasant leaves
That in the springtime shoot:
But grim to see is the gallows-tree,
With its adder-bitten root,
And, green or dry, a man must die
Before it bears its fruit!

The loftiest place is that seat of grace
For which all worldlings try:
But who would stand in hempen band
Upon a scaffold high,
And through a murderer's collar take
His last look at the sky?

It is sweet to dance to violins
When Love and Life are fair:
To dance to flutes, to dance to lutes
Is delicate and rare:
But it is not sweet with nimble feet
To dance upon the air!

So with curious eyes and sick surmise
We watched him day by day,
And wondered if each one of us
Would end the self-same way,
For none can tell to what red Hell
His sightless soul may stray.

At last the dead man walked no more
Amongst the Trial Men,
And I knew that he was standing up
In the black dock's dreadful pen,

And that never would I see his face
In God's sweet world again.

Like two doomed ships that pass in storm
We had crossed each other's way:
But we made no sign, we said no word,
We had no word to say;
For we did not meet in the holy night,
But in the shameful day.

A prison wall was round us both,
Two outcast men we were:
The world had thrust us from its heart,
And God from out His care:
And the iron gin that waits for Sin
Had caught us in its snare.

III
In Debtors' Yard the stones are hard,
And the dripping wall is high,
So it was there he took the air
Beneath the leaden sky,
And by each side a Warder walked,
For fear the man might die.

Or else he sat with those who watched
His anguish night and day;
Who watched him when he rose to weep,
And when he crouched to pray;
Who watched him lest himself should rob
Their scaffold of its prey.

The Governor was strong upon
The Regulations Act:
The Doctor said that Death was but
A scientific fact:
And twice a day the Chaplain called,
And left a little tract.

And twice a day he smoked his pipe,
And drank his quart of beer:
His soul was resolute, and held
No hiding-place for fear;
He often said that he was glad
The hangman's hands were near.

But why he said so strange a thing
No Warder dared to ask:
For he to whom a watcher's doom
Is given as his task,
Must set a lock upon his lips,
And make his face a mask.

Or else he might be moved, and try
To comfort or console:
And what should Human Pity do
Pent up in Murderers' Hole?
What word of grace in such a place
Could help a brother's soul?

With slouch and swing around the ring
We trod the Fools' Parade!
We did not care: we knew we were
The Devil's Own Brigade:

And shaven head and feet of lead
Make a merry masquerade.

We tore the tarry rope to shreds
With blunt and bleeding nails;
We rubbed the doors, and scrubbed the floors,
And cleaned the shining rails:
And, rank by rank, we soaped the plank,
And clattered with the pails.

We sewed the sacks, we broke the stones,
We turned the dusty drill:
We banged the tins, and bawled the hymns,
And sweated on the mill:
But in the heart of every man
Terror was lying still.

So still it lay that every day
Crawled like a weed-clogged wave:
And we forgot the bitter lot
That waits for fool and knave,
Till once, as we tramped in from work,
We passed an open grave.

With yawning mouth the yellow hole
Gaped for a living thing;
The very mud cried out for blood
To the thirsty asphalte ring:
And we knew that ere one dawn grew fair
Some prisoner had to swing.

Right in we went, with soul intent
On Death and Dread and Doom:
The hangman, with his little bag,
Went shuffling through the gloom:
And each man trembled as he crept
Into his numbered tomb.

That night the empty corridors
Were full of forms of Fear,
And up and down the iron town
Stole feet we could not hear,
And through the bars that hide the stars
White faces seemed to peer.

He lay as one who lies and dreams
In a pleasant meadow-land,
The watchers watched him as he slept,
And could not understand
How one could sleep so sweet a sleep
With a hangman close at hand.

But there is no sleep when men must weep
Who never yet have wept:
So we – the fool, the fraud, the knave –
That endless vigil kept,
And through each brain on hands of pain
Another's terror crept.

Alas! it is a fearful thing
To feel another's guilt!
For, right within, the sword of Sin
Pierced to its poisoned hilt,

And as molten lead were the tears we shed
For the blood we had not spilt.

The Warders with their shoes of felt
Crept by each padlocked door,
And peeped and saw, with eyes of awe,
Grey figures on the floor,
And wondered why men knelt to pray
Who never prayed before.

All through the night we knelt and prayed,
Mad mourners of a corpse!
The troubled plumes of midnight were
The plumes upon a hearse:
And bitter wine upon a sponge
Was the savior of Remorse.

The grey cock crew, the red cock crew,
But never came the day:
And crooked shapes of Terror crouched,
In the corners where we lay:
And each evil sprite that walks by night
Before us seemed to play.

They glided past, they glided fast,
Like travellers through a mist:
They mocked the moon in a rigadoon
Of delicate turn and twist,
And with formal pace and loathsome grace
The phantoms kept their tryst.

With mop and mow, we saw them go,
Slim shadows hand in hand:
About, about, in ghostly rout
They trod a saraband:
And the damned grotesques made
    arabesques,
Like the wind upon the sand!

With the pirouettes of marionettes,
They tripped on pointed tread:
But with flutes of Fear they filled the ear,
As their grisly masque they led,
And loud they sang, and long they sang,
For they sang to wake the dead.

'Oho!' they cried, 'The world is wide,
But fettered limbs go lame!
And once, or twice, to throw the dice
Is a gentlemanly game,
But he does not win who plays with Sin
In the secret House of Shame.'

No things of air these antics were,
That frolicked with such glee:
To men whose lives were held in gyves,
And whose feet might not go free,
Ah! wounds of Christ! they were living things,
Most terrible to see.

Around, around, they waltzed and wound;
Some wheeled in smirking pairs;
With the mincing step of a demirep

Some sidled up the stairs:
And with subtle sneer, and fawning leer,
Each helped us at our prayers.

The morning wind began to moan,
But still the night went on:
Through its giant loom the web of gloom
Crept till each thread was spun:
And, as we prayed, we grew afraid
Of the Justice of the Sun.

The moaning wind went wandering round
The weeping prison-wall:
Till like a wheel of turning steel
We felt the minutes crawl:
O moaning wind! what had we done
To have such a seneschal?

At last I saw the shadowed bars,
Like a lattice wrought in lead,
Move right across the whitewashed wall
That faced my three-plank bed,
And I knew that somewhere in the world
God's dreadful dawn was red.

At six o'clock we cleaned our cells,
At seven all was still,
But the sough and swing of a mighty wing
The prison seemed to fill,
For the Lord of Death with icy breath
Had entered in to kill.

He did not pass in purple pomp,
Nor ride a moon-white steed.
Three yards of cord and a sliding board
Are all the gallows' need:
So with rope of shame the Herald came
To do the secret deed.

We were as men who through a fen
Of filthy darkness grope:
We did not dare to breathe a prayer,
Or to give our anguish scope:
Something was dead in each of us,
And what was dead was Hope.

For Man's grim Justice goes its way,
And will not swerve aside:
It slays the weak, it slays the strong,
It has a deadly stride:
With iron heel it slays the strong,
The monstrous parricide!

We waited for the stroke of eight:
Each tongue was thick with thirst:
For the stroke of eight is the stroke of Fate
That makes a man accursed,
And Fate will use a running noose
For the best man and the worst.

We had no other thing to do,
Save to wait for the sign to come:
So, like things of stone in a valley lone,
Quiet we sat and dumb:

But each man's heart beat thick and quick,
Like a madman on a drum!

With sudden shock the prison-clock
Smote on the shivering air,
And from all the gaol rose up a wail
Of impotent despair,
Like the sound that frightened marshes hear
From some leper in his lair.

And as one sees most fearful things
In the crystal of a dream,
We saw the greasy hempen rope
Hooked to the blackened beam,
And heard the prayer the hangman's snare
Strangled into a scream.

And all the woe that moved him so
That he gave that bitter cry,
And the wild regrets, and the bloody sweats,
None knew so well as I:
For he who lives more lives than one
More deaths than one must die.

IV

There is no chapel on the day
On which they hang a man:
The Chaplain's heart is far too sick,
Or his face is far too wan,
Or there is that written in his eyes
Which none should look upon.

So they kept us close till nigh on noon,
And then they rang the bell,
And the Warders with their jingling keys
Opened each listening cell,
And down the iron stair we tramped,
Each from his separate Hell.

Out into God's sweet air we went,
But not in wonted way,
For this man's face was white with fear,
And that man's face was grey,
And I never saw sad men who looked
So wistfully at the day.

I never saw sad men who looked
With such a wistful eye
Upon that little tent of blue
We prisoners called the sky,
And at every careless cloud that passed
In happy freedom by.

But there were those amongst us all
Who walked with downcast head,
And knew that, had each got his due,
They should have died instead:
He had but killed a thing that lived,
Whilst they had killed the dead.

For he who sins a second time
Wakes a dead soul to pain,
And draws it from its spotted shroud,
And makes it bleed again,

And makes it bleed great gouts of blood,
And makes it bleed in vain!

Like ape or clown, in monstrous garb
With crooked arrows starred,
Silently we went round and round
The slippery asphalte yard;
Silently we went round and round,
And no man spoke a word.

Silently we went round and round,
And through each hollow mind
The Memory of dreadful things
Rushed like a dreadful wind,
And Horror stalked before each man,
And Terror crept behind.

The Warders strutted up and down,
And kept their herd of brutes,
Their uniforms were spick and span,
And they wore their Sunday suits,
But we knew the work they had been at,
By the quicklime on their boots.

For where a grave had opened wide,
There was no grave at all:
Only a stretch of mud and sand
By the hideous prison-wall,
And a little heap of burning lime,
That the man should have his pall.

For he has a pall, this wretched man,
Such as few men can claim:
Deep down below a prison-yard,
Naked for greater shame,
He lies, with fetters on each foot,
Wrapt in a sheet of flame!

And all the while the burning lime
Eats flesh and bone away,
It eats the brittle bone by night,
And the soft flesh by day,
It eats the flesh and bone by turns,
But it eats the heart alway.

For three long years they will not sow
Or root or seedling there:
For three long years the unblessed spot
Will sterile be and bare,
And look upon the wondering sky
With unreproachful stare.

They think a murderer's heart would taint
Each simple seed they sow.
It is not true! God's kindly earth
Is kindlier than men know,
And the red rose would but blow
     more red,
The white rose whiter blow.

Out of his mouth a red, red rose!
Out of his heart a white!
For who can say by what strange way,

Christ brings His will to light,
Since the barren staff the pilgrim bore
Bloomed in the great Pope's sight?

But neither milk-white rose nor red
May bloom in prison-air;
The shard, the pebble, and the flint,
Are what they give us there:
For flowers have been known to heal
A common man's despair.

So never will wine-red rose or white,
Petal by petal, fall
On that stretch of mud and sand that lies
By the hideous prison-wall,
To tell the men who tramp the yard
That God's Son died for all.

Yet though the hideous prison-wall
Still hems him round and round,
And a spirit may not walk by night
That is with fetters bound,
And a spirit may but weep that lies
In such unholy ground,

He is at peace – this wretched man –
At peace, or will be soon:
There is no thing to make him mad,
Nor does Terror walk at noon,
For the lampless Earth in which he lies
Has neither Sun nor Moon.

They hanged him as a beast is hanged:
They did not even toll
A requiem that might have brought
Rest to his startled soul,
But hurriedly they took him out,
And hid him in a hole.

They stripped him of his canvas clothes,
And gave him to the flies:
They mocked the swollen purple throat,
And the stark and staring eyes:
And with laughter loud they heaped the shroud
In which their convict lies.

The Chaplain would not kneel to pray
By his dishonoured grave:
Nor mark it with that blessed Cross
That Christ for sinners gave,
Because the man was one of those
Whom Christ came down to save.

Yet all is well; he has but passed
To Life's appointed bourne:
And alien tears will fill for him
Pity's long-broken urn,
For his mourners will be outcast men,
And outcasts always mourn

V

I know not whether Laws be right,
Or whether Laws be wrong;
All that we know who lie in gaol

Is that the wall is strong;
And that each day is like a year,
A year whose days are long.

But this I know, that every Law
That men have made for Man,
Since first Man took his brother's life,
And the sad world began,
But straws the wheat and saves the chaff
With a most evil fan.

This too I know – and wise it were
If each could know the same –
That every prison that men build
Is built with bricks of shame,
And bound with bars lest Christ should see
How men their brothers maim.

With bars they blur the gracious moon,
And blind the goodly sun:
And they do well to hide their Hell,
For in it things are done
That Son of God nor son of Man
Ever should look upon!

The vilest deeds like poison weeds,
Bloom well in prison-air;
It is only what is good in Man
That wastes and withers there:
Pale Anguish keeps the heavy gate,
And the Warder is Despair.

For they starve the little frightened child
Till it weeps both night and day:
And they scourge the weak, and flog the fool,
And gibe the old and grey,
And some grow mad, and all grow bad,
And none a word may say.

Each narrow cell in which we dwell
Is a foul and dark latrine,
And the fetid breath of living Death
Chokes up each grated screen,
And all, but Lust, is turned to dust
In Humanity's machine.

The brackish water that we drink
Creeps with a loathsome slime,
And the bitter bread they weigh in scales
Is full of chalk and lime,
And Sleep will not lie down, but walks
Wild-eyed, and cries to Time.

But though lean Hunger and green Thirst
Like asp with adder fight,
We have little care of prison fare,
For what chills and kills outright
Is that every stone one lifts by day
Becomes one's heart by night.

With midnight always in one's heart,
And twilight in one's cell,
We turn the crank, or tear the rope,
Each in his separate Hell,

And the silence is more awful far
Than the sound of a brazen bell.

And never a human voice comes near
To speak a gentle word:
And the eye that watches through the door
Is pitiless and hard:
And by all forgot, we rot and rot,
With soul and body marred.

And thus we rust Life's iron chain
Degraded and alone:
And some men curse, and some men weep,
And some men make no moan:
But God's eternal Laws are kind
And break the heart of stone.

And every human heart that breaks,
In prison-cell or yard,
Is as that broken box that gave
Its treasure to the Lord,
And filled the unclean leper's house
With the scent of costliest nard.

Ah! happy they whose hearts can break
And peace of pardon win!
How else may man make straight his plan
And cleanse his soul from Sin?
How else but through a broken heart
May Lord Christ enter in?

And he of the swollen purple throat,
And the stark and staring eyes,
Waits for the holy hands that took
The Thief to Paradise;
And a broken and a contrite heart
The Lord will not despise.

The man in red who reads the Law
Gave him three weeks of life,
Three little weeks in which to heal
His soul of his soul's strife,
And cleanse from every blot of blood
The hand that held the knife.

And with tears of blood he cleansed the hand,
The hand that held the steel:
For only blood can wipe out blood,
And only tears can heal:
And the crimson stain that was of Cain
Became Christ's snow-white seal.

VI

In Reading gaol by Reading town
There is a pit of shame,
And in it lies a wretched man
Eaten by teeth of flame,
In a burning winding-sheet he lies,
And his grave has got no name.

And there, till Christ call forth the dead,
In silence let him lie:
No need to waste the foolish tear,

Or heave the windy sigh:
The man had killed the thing he loved,
And so he had to die.

And all men kill the thing they love,
By all let this be heard,
Some do it with a bitter look,
Some with a flattering word,
The coward does it with a kiss,
The brave man with a sword!

Ravenna

I

A year ago I breathed the Italian air, –
And yet, methinks this northern Spring is fair, –
These fields made golden with the flower of March,
The throstle singing on the feathered larch,
The cawing rooks, the wood-doves fluttering by,
The little clouds that race across the sky;
And fair the violet's gentle drooping head,
The primrose, pale for love uncomforted,
The rose that burgeons on the climbing briar,
The crocus-bed, (that seems a moon of fire
Round-girdled with a purple marriage-ring);
And all the flowers of our English Spring,
Fond snowdrops, and the bright-starred daffodil.
Up starts the lark beside the murmuring mill,
And breaks the gossamer-threads of early dew;
And down the river, like a flame of blue,
Keen as an arrow flies the water-king,
While the brown linnets in the greenwood sing.
A year ago! – it seems a little time
Since last I saw that lordly southern clime,
Where flower and fruit to purple radiance blow,
And like bright lamps the fabled apples glow.
Full Spring it was – and by rich flowering vines,
Dark olive-groves and noble forest-pines,
I rode at will; the moist glad air was sweet,
The white road rang beneath my horse's feet,
And musing on Ravenna's ancient name,
I watched the day till, marked with wounds of flame,
The turquoise sky to burnished gold was turned.

O how my heart with boyish passion burned,
When far away across the sedge and mere
I saw that Holy City rising clear,
Crowned with her crown of towers! – On
　　and on
I galloped, racing with the setting sun,
And ere the crimson after-glow was passed,
I stood within Ravenna's walls at last!

II

How strangely still! no sound of life or joy
Startles the air; no laughing shepherd-boy
Pipes on his reed, nor ever through the day
Comes the glad sound of children at their play:
O sad, and sweet, and silent! surely here
A man might dwell apart from troublous fear,
Watching the tide of seasons as they flow
From amorous Spring to Winter's rain and snow,
And have no thought of sorrow; – here, indeed,
Are Lethe's waters, and that fatal weed
Which makes a man forget his fatherland.

Ay! amid lotus-meadows dost thou stand,
Like Proserpine, with poppy-laden head,
Guarding the holy ashes of the dead.
For though thy brood of warrior sons hath
　　ceased,
Thy noble dead are with thee! – they at least
Are faithful to thine honour: – guard them well,
O childless city! for a mighty spell,
To wake men's hearts to dreams of things sublime,
Are the lone tombs where rest the Great of Time.

III

Yon lonely pillar, rising on the plain,
Marks where the bravest knight of France was slain, –
The Prince of chivalry, the Lord of war,
Gaston de Foix: for some untimely star
Led him against thy city, and he fell,
As falls some forest-lion fighting well.
Taken from life while life and love were new,
He lies beneath God's seamless veil of blue;
Tall lance-like reeds wave sadly o'er his head,
And oleanders bloom to deeper red,
Where his bright youth flowed crimson on the ground.

Look farther north unto that broken mound, –
There, prisoned now within a lordly tomb
Raised by a daughter's hand, in lonely gloom,
Huge-limbed Theodoric, the Gothic king,
Sleeps after all his weary conquering.
Time hath not spared his ruin, – wind and rain
Have broken down his stronghold; and again
We see that Death is mighty lord of all,
And king and clown to ashen dust must fall

Mighty indeed THEIR glory! yet to me
Barbaric king, or knight of chivalry,
Or the great queen herself, were poor and vain,
Beside the grave where Dante rests from pain.
His gilded shrine lies open to the air;
And cunning sculptor's hands have carven there
The calm white brow, as calm as earliest morn,
The eyes that flashed with passionate love and scorn,
The lips that sang of Heaven and of Hell,

The almond-face which Giotto drew so well,
The weary face of Dante; – to this day,
Here in his place of resting, far away
From Arno's yellow waters, rushing down
Through the wide bridges of that fairy town,
Where the tall tower of Giotto seems to rise
A marble lily under sapphire skies!

Alas! my Dante! thou hast known the pain
Of meaner lives, – the exile's galling chain,
How steep the stairs within kings' houses are,
And all the petty miseries which mar
Man's nobler nature with the sense of wrong.
Yet this dull world is grateful for thy song;
Our nations do thee homage, – even she,
That cruel queen of vine-clad Tuscany,
Who bound with crown of thorns thy living
    brow,
Hath decked thine empty tomb with laurels now,
And begs in vain the ashes of her son.

O mightiest exile! all thy grief is done:
Thy soul walks now beside thy Beatrice;
Ravenna guards thine ashes: sleep in peace.

IV
How lone this palace is; how grey the walls!
No minstrel now wakes echoes in these halls.
The broken chain lies rusting on the door,
And noisome weeds have split the marble floor:
Here lurks the snake, and here the lizards run
By the stone lions blinking in the sun.

Byron dwelt here in love and revelry
For two long years – a second Anthony,
Who of the world another Actium made!
Yet suffered not his royal soul to fade,
Or lyre to break, or lance to grow less keen,
'Neath any wiles of an Egyptian queen.
For from the East there came a mighty cry,
And Greece stood up to fight for Liberty,
And called him from Ravenna: never knight
Rode forth more nobly to wild scenes of fight!
None fell more bravely on ensanguined field,
Borne like a Spartan back upon his shield!
O Hellas! Hellas! in thine hour of pride,
Thy day of might, remember him who died
To wrest from off thy limbs the trammelling chain:
O Salamis! O lone Plataean plain!
O tossing waves of wild Euboean sea!
O wind-swept heights of lone Thermopylae!
He loved you well – ay, not alone in word,
Who freely gave to thee his lyre and sword,
Like Æschylos at well-fought Marathon:

And England, too, shall glory in her son,
Her warrior-poet, first in song and fight.
No longer now shall Slander's venomed spite
Crawl like a snake across his perfect name,
Or mar the lordly scutcheon of his fame.

For as the olive-garland of the race,
Which lights with joy each eager runner's face,
As the red cross which saveth men in war,
As a flame-bearded beacon seen from far

By mariners upon a storm-tossed sea, –
Such was his love for Greece and Liberty!

Byron, thy crowns are ever fresh and green:
Red leaves of rose from Sapphic Mitylene
Shall bind thy brows; the myrtle blooms for thee,
In hidden glades by lonely Castaly;
The laurels wait thy coming: all are thine,
And round thy head one perfect wreath will twine.

V

The pine-tops rocked before the evening breeze
With the hoarse murmur of the wintry seas,
And the tall stems were streaked with amber bright; –
I wandered through the wood in wild delight,
Some startled bird, with fluttering wings and fleet,
Made snow of all the blossoms; at my feet,
Like silver crowns, the pale narcissi lay,
And small birds sang on every twining spray.
O waving trees, O forest liberty!
Within your haunts at least a man is free,
And half forgets the weary world of strife:
The blood flows hotter, and a sense of life
Wakes i' the quickening veins, while once again
The woods are filled with gods we fancied slain.
Long time I watched, and surely hoped to see
Some goat-foot Pan make merry minstrelsy
Amid the reeds! some startled Dryad-maid
In girlish flight! or lurking in the glade,
The soft brown limbs, the wanton treacherous face
Of woodland god! Queen Dian in the chase,
White-limbed and terrible, with look of pride,

And leash of boar-hounds leaping at her side!
Or Hylas mirrored in the perfect stream.

O idle heart! O fond Hellenic dream!
Ere long, with melancholy rise and swell,
The evening chimes, the convent's vesper bell,
Struck on mine ears amid the amorous flowers.
Alas! alas! these sweet and honied hours
Had whelmed my heart like some encroaching sea,
And drowned all thoughts of black Gethsemane.

VI

O lone Ravenna! many a tale is told
Of thy great glories in the days of old:
Two thousand years have passed since thou didst see
Caesar ride forth to royal victory.
Mighty thy name when Rome's lean eagles flew
From Britain's isles to far Euphrates blue;
And of the peoples thou wast noble queen,
Till in thy streets the Goth and Hun were seen.
Discrowned by man, deserted by the sea,
Thou sleepest, rocked in lonely misery!
No longer now upon thy swelling tide,
Pine-forest-like, thy myriad galleys ride!
For where the brass-beaked ships were wont to float,
The weary shepherd pipes his mournful note;
And the white sheep are free to come and go
Where Adria's purple waters used to flow.

O fair! O sad! O Queen uncomforted!
In ruined loveliness thou liest dead,
Alone of all thy sisters; for at last

Italia's royal warrior hath passed
Rome's lordliest entrance, and hath worn his crown
In the high temples of the Eternal Town!
The Palatine hath welcomed back her king,
And with his name the seven mountains ring!

And Naples hath outlived her dream of pain,
And mocks her tyrant! Venice lives again,
New risen from the waters! and the cry
Of Light and Truth, of Love and Liberty,
Is heard in lordly Genoa, and where
The marble spires of Milan wound the air,
Rings from the Alps to the Sicilian shore,
And Dante's dream is now a dream no more.

But thou, Ravenna, better loved than all,
Thy ruined palaces are but a pall
That hides thy fallen greatness! and thy name
Burns like a grey and flickering candle-flame
Beneath the noonday splendour of the sun
Of new Italia! for the night is done,
The night of dark oppression, and the day
Hath dawned in passionate splendour: far away
The Austrian hounds are hunted from the land,
Beyond those ice-crowned citadels which stand
Girdling the plain of royal Lombardy,
From the far West unto the Eastern sea.

I know, indeed, that sons of thine have died
In Lissa's waters, by the mountain-side
Of Aspromonte, on Novara's plain, –
Nor have thy children died for thee in vain:

And yet, methinks, thou hast not drunk this wine
From grapes new-crushed of Liberty divine,
Thou hast not followed that immortal Star
Which leads the people forth to deeds of war.
Weary of life, thou liest in silent sleep,
As one who marks the lengthening shadows creep,
Careless of all the hurrying hours that run,
Mourning some day of glory, for the sun
Of Freedom hath not shewn to thee his face,
And thou hast caught no flambeau in the race.

Yet wake not from thy slumbers, – rest thee well,
Amidst thy fields of amber asphodel,
Thy lily-sprinkled meadows, – rest thee there,
To mock all human greatness: who would dare
To vent the paltry sorrows of his life
Before thy ruins, or to praise the strife
Of kings' ambition, and the barren pride
Of warring nations! wert not thou the Bride
Of the wild Lord of Adria's stormy sea!
The Queen of double Empires! and to thee
Were not the nations given as thy prey!
And now – thy gates lie open night and day,
The grass grows green on every tower and hall,
The ghastly fig hath cleft thy bastioned wall;
And where thy mailed warriors stood at rest
The midnight owl hath made her secret nest.
O fallen! fallen! from thy high estate,
O city trammelled in the toils of Fate,
Doth nought remain of all thy glorious days,
But a dull shield, a crown of withered bays!
Yet who beneath this night of wars and fears,

From tranquil tower can watch the coming years;
Who can foretell what joys the day shall bring,
Or why before the dawn the linnets sing?
Thou, even thou, mayst wake, as wakes the rose
To crimson splendour from its grave of snows;
As the rich corn-fields rise to red and gold
From these brown lands, now stiff with Winter's cold;
As from the storm-rack comes a perfect star!

O much-loved city! I have wandered far
From the wave-circled islands of my home;
Have seen the gloomy mystery of the Dome
Rise slowly from the drear Campagna's way,
Clothed in the royal purple of the day:
I from the city of the violet crown
Have watched the sun by Corinth's hill go down,
And marked the 'myriad laughter' of the sea
From starlit hills of flower-starred Arcady;
Yet back to thee returns my perfect love,
As to its forest-nest the evening dove.

O poet's city! one who scarce has seen
Some twenty summers cast their doublets green
For Autumn's livery, would seek in vain
To wake his lyre to sing a louder strain,
Or tell thy days of glory; – poor indeed
Is the low murmur of the shepherd's reed,
Where the loud clarion's blast should shake the sky,
And flame across the heavens! and to try
Such lofty themes were folly: yet I know
That never felt my heart a nobler glow
Than when I woke the silence of thy street

With clamorous trampling of my horse's feet,
And saw the city which now I try to sing,
After long days of weary travelling.

VII

Adieu, Ravenna! but a year ago,
I stood and watched the crimson sunset glow
From the lone chapel on thy marshy plain:
The sky was as a shield that caught the stain
Of blood and battle from the dying sun,
And in the west the circling clouds had spun
A royal robe, which some great God might wear,
While into ocean-seas of purple air
Sank the gold galley of the Lord of Light.

Yet here the gentle stillness of the night
Brings back the swelling tide of memory,
And wakes again my passionate love for thee:
Now is the Spring of Love, yet soon will come
On meadow and tree the Summer's lordly bloom;
And soon the grass with brighter flowers will blow,
And send up lilies for some boy to mow.
Then before long the Summer's conqueror,
Rich Autumn-time, the season's usurer,
Will lend his hoarded gold to all the trees,
And see it scattered by the spendthrift breeze;
And after that the Winter cold and drear.
So runs the perfect cycle of the year.
And so from youth to manhood do we go,
And fall to weary days and locks of snow.
Love only knows no winter; never dies:
Nor cares for frowning storms or leaden skies

And mine for thee shall never pass away,
Though my weak lips may falter in my lay.

Adieu! Adieu! yon silent evening star,
The night's ambassador, doth gleam afar,
And bid the shepherd bring his flocks to fold.
Perchance before our inland seas of gold
Are garnered by the reapers into sheaves,
Perchance before I see the Autumn leaves,
I may behold thy city; and lay down
Low at thy feet the poet's laurel crown.

Adieu! Adieu! yon silver lamp, the moon,
Which turns our midnight into perfect noon,
Doth surely light thy towers, guarding well
Where Dante sleeps, where Byron loved to dwell.

Index of First Lines

A lily girl, not made for this world's pain   69

A ring of gold and milk-white dove   81

A year ago I breathed the Italian air   223

Albeit nurtured in democracy   22

As oftentimes the too resplendent sun   142

As one who poring on a Grecian urn   128

Christ, dost Thou live indeed? Or are Thy bones   20

Come down, O Christ, and help me! reach Thy hand   51

Could we dig up this long-buried treasure   178

Dear Heart, I think the young impassioned priest   141

Eagle of Austerlitz! where thy wings   19

He did not wear his scarlet coat   198

He was a Grecian lad, who coming home   82

Her ivory hands on the ivory keys   114

How steep the stairs within Kings' houses are   138

How vain and dull this common world must seem   127

I am weary of lying within the chase   115

I can write no stately proem   177

I have no store   174

I reached the Alps: the soul within me burned   36

I stood by the unvintageable sea   67

I wandered in Scoglietto's green retreat   43

In a dim corner of my room for longer than my fancy thinks   184

In the glad springtime when leaves were green   165

Is it thy will that I should wax and wane 139

It is full summer now, the heart of June 23

It is full winter now: the trees are bare 147

Italia! thou art fallen, though with sheen 42

Like burnt-out torches by a sick man's bed 125

Milton! I think thy spirit hath passed away 18

My limbs are wasted with a flame 79

Nay, let us walk from fire unto fire 129

Nay, Lord, not thus! white lilies in the spring 49

Not that I love thy children, whose dull eyes 12

O beautiful star with the crimson mouth! 167

O goat-foot God of Arcady! 182

O singer of Persephone! 113

Oft have we trod the vales of Castaly 120

Out of the mid-wood's twilight 176

Rid of the world's injustice, and his pain 112

Rome! What a scroll of History thine has been! 48

See, I have climbed the mountain side 37

Seven stars in the still water 118

Set in this stormy Northern sea 13

The apple trees are hung with gold 77

The corn has turned from grey to red 39

The Gods are dead: no longer do we bring 121

The little white clouds are racing over the sky 70

The oleander on the wall   123

The sea is flecked with bars of grey   110

The sea was sapphire coloured, and the sky   124

The seasons send their ruin as they go   181

The silent room, the heavy creeping shade   126

The silver trumpets rang across the Dome: 50

The sin was mine; I did not understand   173

The sky is laced with fitful red   137

The Thames nocturne of blue and gold   68

The western wind is blowing fair   75

The wild bee reels from bough to bough   143

There was a time in Europe long ago   21

These are the letters which Endymion wrote   172

This English Thames is holier far than Rome   52

This mighty empire hath but feet of clay   34

This winter air is keen and cold   171

Thou knowest all; I seek in vain   166

To drift with every passion till my soul   11

To stab my youth with desperate knife, to wear   146

To that gaunt House of Art which lacks for naught   72

Tread lightly, she is near   35

Two crowned Kings and One that stood alone   122

Was this His coming! I had hoped to see   38

We caught the tread of dancing feet   169

Where hast thou been since round the walls of Troy   44

Within this restless, hurried, modern world   145